Happiness:
Finding Inner Peace and Contentment

by Gopi Vishnu, Ph.D

NMD Books
Simi Valley, CA

Copyright 2011 –Gopi Vishnu

All rights reserved. No part of this book may be reproduced in any format or by any means without written permission from the publisher

Visit our Web site at http://www.NMDbooks.com.

Happiness: Finding Inner Peace and Contentment
by Gopi Vishnu, PH.D

Library of Congress Cataloging-in-Publication Data

ISBN978-1-936828-14-2 (Softcover)

First Edition January 2011

INTRODUCTION

What is inner peace and contentment? Throughout the ages man has sought to attain this state of mind or state of being.

It is without question the very essence of happiness, the sense of well being and satisfaction that is free of anxiety, worry and stress.

No amount of material wealth, power or any other outside pursuit can seem to manifest this most elusive of states, yet many of us seem to think that they will.

With all the progress we have made, one would think mankind would have found the answer to the many riddles of existence; at the very least we would have found a way out of our mental suffering and distress.

But, it appears it is just the opposite.

With all of our technology, advances and our vast accumulation of knowledge, we are still plagued by the same question that has dogged man since the dawn of time: how do I attain true happiness?

How do I rid myself of the fear, the worry, the suffering, the pain that seems to come from the simple act of living itself?

The answer to this question remains the most elusive of all things.

Of course, happiness means many things to many people. But the end result that people seek is a feeling of deep inner peace; of balance; of the feeling that they are in the exact right place in time, in the moment.

The state of contentment is what we seek.

Yet, we are so restless, all the time it seems. The mind races from one thought to the next, one imagined stressor to another, while the body responds with elevated testosterone levels, increased heart rates and over worked adrenal glands.

The result is a litany of health problems, both mental and physical. High blood pressure, arteriosclerosis, diabetes, and yes, even compromised brain function that can lead to actual neuron and brain damage.

Why are we so stressed?

Much of it is because our fight or flight response systems are getting false information from our conscious and subconscious minds that we are in danger – although we are really not.

It is an imagined thing – and our nervous systems are unable to distinguish between a real or an imagined threat.

Worse yet, and we cannot seem to turn it off.

Many scientists believe we have not yet evolved from our old places in the animal kingdom.

How do we condition ourselves to at least cope better with our genetic dilemma?

Thankfully we have a wealth of information we can draw on in stress reduction studies that point to methods we can use to achieve inner states of well being, happiness and contentment.

Very often times we place ourselves in stressful situations that can best be avoided, and when we can't do that, we must learn ways to cope with stress.

Beyond that, we must actively pursue methods and lifestyles that promote our own happiness, and as it turns out, this will greatly improve the well being and happiness of those within our orbit.

Where do we start?

We start right now, in the moment of Now.

In the moment living is really the true essence of happiness. Much of the research and studies show that people who maintain a state of mind that is focused on the present, "supremely in the moment," without regard of thoughts of the future or pre-occupied with memories from the past, can one be truly at one with themselves and the surrounding universe.

This means being free of present worries and anxiety, if but for only a few moments at a time, to rise above the seemingly threatening pressing problems that occur in our everyday lives.

Stress reduction is a learned behavior and is the first step toward allowing our minds and bodies to release the tension that blocks us from relaxation, and ultimately inner peace.

The state of inner peace and contentment is largely a physiological one, yet has a vital mental component that must work in tandem with the body.

This book will help you to achieve that balance, and lead a more fulfilling life, one with purpose, meaning and true happiness.

Gopi Vishnu
Los Angeles
2011

"He is happiest who confines his wants to natural necessities; and he that goes further in his desires, increases his wants in proportion to his acquisitions."

- Richard Steele, Journalist (1709)

Table of Contents:

Happiness Defined	9
Ego and It's Affect On Happiness	14
Physiological Aspects of Happiness	15
Brain and Body Chemistry	18
Sleeping and Dreaming	22
Rest and Relaxation	26
Mind Awareness: Mental Aspects of Happiness	27
Sense Pleasure Happiness (and Why It Doesn't Last)	33
The "If Only" Delusion	34
Everything You Need To Be Happy You Already Possess	34
Money and Happiness (They Aren't Related)	35
Stress Factors	37
Noise Pollution	45
Stress While Driving	52
Dealing With Difficult People and Avoiding Conflict	55
Reading - The Beginning Of Liberation	58
The Practice of Happiness	58
9 Habits of Happy People	59
Being In The 'Now' - This Moment Is All We Have	64
The Objective Observer - Lose Your Identification with Self	67
Helping Others	70
Freeing The Mind	74
Getting Outside the Self and Ego	76
Getting Past The Ego	78
Faith	80
The Importance of Community	88
What is My Purpose?	90
Getting Involved	91
Mental Exercises	92
Meditation - Visualization - Freeing The Mind	94
Physical Excercises for Stress Relief	96
Music - How Relaxation Music Works	99
Humor Therapy - How A Funny Outlook Can Free You	100
Movies and TV - Input Affects Output - What You Watch, Listen to and Experience Makes A Difference	104
Pursuing Happiness Each Day	105
Recommended Reading:	106
Stress Relieving Music:	106
Recommended Websites:	106

Happiness Defined

Happiness is a very fuzzy concept and can mean many things to many people. Part of the challenge of the science of happiness is to identify all the different uses of the word "happiness", or else to understand its various components.

Webster's defines Happiness as:

a : a state of well-being and contentment : joy
b : a pleasurable or satisfying

Studies have found that things like money, education, or the weather do not affect happiness the way one might expect. There are various habits that have been correlated with happiness.

Psychologist Martin Seligman provides the acronym PERMA to summarize many of Positive Psychology's findings; humans seem happiest when they have Pleasure (tasty foods, warm baths, etc.), Engagement or (aka Flow, the absorption of an enjoyed yet challenging activity), Relationships (social ties have turned out to be extremely reliable indicator of happiness), Meaning (a perceived quest or belonging to something bigger), and finally Accomplishments (having realized tangible goals).

There is evidence suggesting that people can improve their happiness. Mood disorders like depression are often understood through a Biopsychosocial model, meaning biological, psychological, and social factors all contribute to mood (i.e. there is no single cause).

The Diathesis-stress model further argues that a diathesis (a biological vulnerability- due to genes) to certain moods are worsened or improved by the environment and upbringing.

The idea is that individuals with high vulnerability, especially if their early environment worsened depressive tendencies, may need Antidepressants. Furthermore, the model suggests that everyone can benefit, to varying degrees, from the various habits and practices identified by Positive psychology.

There has also been some studies of religion as it relates to happiness, as well as religious or generally philosophical notions of happiness. Research has generally found that religion may help make people happier by providing various important components (e.g. PERMA) in countries where there are many who share that religion.

Several religious perspectives give us slightly differing viewpoints in the definition of happiness.

Happiness forms a central theme of Buddhist teachings. For ultimate freedom from suffering, the Noble Eightfold Path leads its practitioner to Nirvana, a state of everlasting peace. Ultimate happiness is only achieved by overcoming craving in all forms.

More mundane forms of happiness, such as acquiring wealth and maintaining good friendships, are also recognized as worthy goals for lay people (see sukha). Buddhism also encourages the generation of loving kindness and compassion, the desire for the happiness and welfare of all beings.

In Catholicism, the ultimate end of human existence consists in felicity (Latin equivalent to the Greek eudaimonia), or "blessed happiness", described by the 13th-century philosopher-theologian Thomas Aquinas as a Beatific Vision of God's essence in the next life.

The Chinese Confucian thinker Mencius, who 2300 years ago sought to give advice to the ruthless political leaders of the warring states period, was convinced that the mind played a mediating role between the "lesser self" (the physiological self) and the "greater self" (the moral self) and that getting the priorities right between these two would lead to sage-hood.

He argued that if we did not feel satisfaction or pleasure in nourishing one's "vital force" with "righteous deeds", that force would shrivel up (Mencius,6A:15 2A:2). More specifically, he mentions the experience of intoxicating joy if one celebrates the practice of the great virtues, especially through music.

Al-Ghazali (1058–1111) the Muslim Sufi thinker wrote the Alchemy of Happiness, a manual of spiritual instruction throughout the Muslim world and widely practiced today.

The Hindu thinker Patanjali, author of the Yoga Sutras, wrote quite exhaustively on the psychological and ontological roots of bliss.

In the Nicomachean Ethics, written in 350 BCE, Aristotle stated that happiness (also being well and doing well) is the only thing that humans desire for its own sake, unlike riches, honor, health or friendship. He observed that men sought riches, or honor, or health not only for their own sake but also in order to be happy.

Note that eudaimonia, the term we translate as "happiness", is for Aristotle an activity rather than an emotion or a state.[8] Happiness is characteristic of a good life, that is, a life in which a person fulfills human nature in an excellent way. People have a set of purposes which are typically human: these belong to our nature.

The happy person is virtuous, meaning they have outstanding abilities and emotional tendencies which allow him or her to fulfill our common human ends.
For Aristotle, then, happiness is "the virtuous activity of the soul in accordance with reason": happiness is the practice of virtue.

Many ethicists make arguments for how humans should behave, either individually or collectively, based on the resulting happiness of such behavior. Utilitarians, such as John Stuart Mill and Jeremy Bentham, advocated the greatest happiness principle as a guide for ethical behavior.

Positive Feelings and Positive Activities
Dr. Martin Seligman, one of the founders of positive psychology, uses happiness and well-being interchangeably. His definition of happiness is: both positive feelings (such as ecstasy and comfort) and positive activities that have no feeling component at all (such as absorption and engagement). In his happy life formula, Dr. Seligman defines a happy life as a life filled with positive feelings and activities. he says the degree to which you experience these feelings most of the time is your level of enduring happiness.

The Fuel To Thrive and Flourish
Another positive psychologist, Dr. Barbara Fredrickson, defines happiness as, the fuel to thrive and to flourish, and to leave this world in better shape than you found it. Like Dr. Seligman, she believes that happiness includes activities that are absorbing and engaging. She goes on to say, You tap into it whenever you feel energized and excited by new ideas. You tap into it whenever you feel at one with your surroundings, at peace. You tap into it whenever you feel playful, creative, or silly. You tap into it whenever you feel your soul stirred by the sheer beauty of existence. You tap into it whenever you feel connected to others and loved. In short, you tap into it whenever positive emotions resonate within you.

A Genuine Smile
Guillaume Duchenne, an early happiness researcher, looked at the quality of people's smiles and found that truly happy people had a smile that not only turned up the corners of their mouths, but also crinkled the skin around their eyes. Studies of year book photos showed that people who had these genuine smiles consistently had higher life satisfaction than those that didn't smile genuinely. So, another definition of happiness is a genuine smile that includes your eyes.

Good Physiology
Happiness can also be defined by our physiology. Researchers can identify happy people by their brain waves, their predominant hormones, and by the chemical make up of their cells . As people's moods shift from tense to happy, researchers can measure changes in blood pressure, heart beat and circulation. The Institute of Heart Math studies variability in heart rate and finds that people who are feeling happy have very regular heart beats while those who are stressed or unhappy have irregular heart beats. They use this pattern to create biofeedback machines that help people learn how to develop happier thought and behavior patterns. All of these physiological markers show researchers that feeling happy has definite benefits for our bodies and each marker becomes a definition of happiness.

Peace and Contentment
Another authority on happiness, the Dalai Lama, says that Happiness is determined more by the state of one's mind than by one's external conditions, circumstances or events- at least once one's basic survival needs are met. This state of mind is characterized by feelings of peace and contentment and manifests itself as acts of compassion towards others.

Thoughts and Emotions Are Not Reality
We spend all our time embroiled in our thoughts and emotions. We think thoughts and emotions are the real self. But thoughts and emotions are simply like clouds passing by in the open, clear space of our original mind. Sometimes the clouds are white and puffy. Sometimes they are stormy. But they are never permanent, nor are they our true essence. All our suffering comes from confusing the clouds for the sky and holding on to them ever so tightly.

Building Blocks of Happiness
In her book, Happy For No Reason, Marci Shimoff agrees with the Dalai Lama that happiness is a state of mind more than a reflection of circumstances. She defines a spectrum of happiness

moving from unhappy to happy for bad reason (like alcohol or drugs) to happy for good reason (like love, accomplishment, or engagement in interesting activities) to happy for no reason. Happy for no reason is a state of mind that is open, expansive and friendly no matter what the circumstances.

What ever method you use to define happiness, Miriam Webster got it right when they declared that the definition of happiness as good fortune is becoming obsolete. Although the origin of the word happiness came from luck or good fortune, this definition is obsolete because we humans now know the keys to happiness and we can learn to enhance our happiness at any time. We no longer need to rely solely on luck to experience joy.

Ego and It's Affect On Happiness

Ego as we define it here means *'identification with form.'*

The essence of who we really are is not the identity we associate ourselves with. Often we see ourselves as (identify with) the roles we play in life.

For instance, a housewife sees herself as a housewife and identifies all of her thoughts and feelings with that role. A corporate president sees himself as the boss, in power and control, a decision maker who runs the company, and sees himself as being that role.

But who we are, the essence of our spirit, is not the identity we associate ourselves with. The "I", "Mine," or "Me" in our awareness is the thing that often is the cause of our suffering and unhappiness.

Very often the cause of our discomfort and dissonance when we feel unhappy or the twinges of unhappiness is a perceived affront or disappointment of an unmet expectation we have set up in our minds.

Someone has disappointed us, let us down. Or our employer has not given us an expected or deserved raise or promotion. Perhaps a stock we have invested in that we expected would yield dividends, plummets.

The list of things which cause our unhappiness is almost endless, as endless as our list of wants, desires and perceived needs and expectations.

What is needed is not a way to change our environment, social status or wealth, but a way to manage our expectations and perceived wants and needs, and to understand the things which make us unhappy are often illusions of the mind.

This is a simple shift in perception, but quite difficult to achieve when we have a lifetime of conditioning to re-program.

Our entire society is based on the wealth and success model, and "getting our due," being success-driven and achieving wealth and beauty are so valued and so well-entrenched as our model to achieve happiness that we don't see the mass delusion and the endless suffering this value system has caused.

Although this basic value system is at the heart of happiness (and perceived unhappiness), there are other factors which affect it. First let's explore some of the physiological aspects of happiness.

Physiological Aspects of Happiness

Positive emotions and the brain

Is there a biological dimension to happiness? Why does your heart seem to "jump for joy" or your eyes "light up" when you feel happy? Researchers now agree that there is a biomolecular aspect to happiness and that the brain is command central for the chemical and physiological changes that occur in the body with positive emotions. While many researchers have studied positive emotions by observing human and animal behavior, others are trying to discover what is happening inside the brain at the structural and molecular levels.

Since the middle of the 20th century, neuroscientists have investigated the mechanisms of positive emotion in the brain and body. Before that time, positive emotions were regarded as too subjective for rigorous scientific study. But a better understanding of the brain chemicals known as neurotransmitters and increased ability to use technology to create images of the living brain opened new opportunities for study.

In the 1950s, psychologists identified a "pleasure center" in an area of the brain known as the nucleus accumbens. They found that laboratory animals would press a lever to deliver an electrical stimulus to their own brain's "pleasure center" repeatedly until they were exhausted—undeterred by hunger, thirst, or pain. When researchers stimulate the nucleus accumbens of people, they smile, laugh, and report feeling pleasure, happiness, or euphoria. Later, by mapping connected areas, the researchers identified a reward circuit in the brain that involves the prefrontal cortex (the thinking part of the brain) and several underlying areas, including the nucleus accumbens and the amygdala.

The chemical basis of these pleasurable sensations also came under investigation. While the interactions are extremely complex and variable, some patterns have been described. Researchers found that the neurotransmitter dopamine activates the reward system and is associated with positive emotions, exuberance, and desire. On the downside, the dopamine reward system may also be associated with addictions, in which people develop uncontrollable urges to repeatedly engage in pleasurable but harmful behaviors, ranging from taking drugs to gambling excessively.

Another group of chemicals, the internally produced opiate-like chemicals called endorphins, are also associated with pleasurable feelings, such as those created by eating chocolate or a runner's high. Endorphins released in the brain also increase the release of dopamine.

When people feel happy, they often feel physical sensations—a rush of passion, a flutter of joy—that correspond to brain signals to nerves of the heart, circulatory system, skin, and muscles. These physical sensations are accompanied by chemical changes in the brain and are interpreted as pleasurable.

Scientists have used modern brain imaging methods to help determine exactly which areas of the brain correspond to sensations of pleasure. This approach has revealed distinct patterns in both the cortex and underlying structures when people feel negative and positive emotions. In the 1990s, researchers used positron emission tomography (PET) scans to produce three-dimensional images of people's working brains. They observed that positive and negative emotions activated different parts of the brain, and that areas activated by happiness were deactivated by sadness and vice versa.

Another technique, electroencephalography, revealed striking, emotionally-based asymmetries in the activity of the prefrontal cortex. In these studies, the brains of generally happy people showed greater activity in the left prefrontal cortex, and this area became more active when people were exposed to amusing video clips. The right side, on the other hand, became more active when people experienced negative emotions.

The development of a new brain imaging technology, functional magnetic resonance imaging (fMRI), spurred a large increase in the number of brain studies, contributing to some confusion about which areas of the brain were associated with happiness and sadness. Results of these many studies suggest that the brain may be even more complex than once imagined by earlier researchers. Nonetheless, many studies support the notion that the left side of the brain is generally associated with positive emotions and the right side with negative emotions. They have also identified the anterior cingulate cortex as active in emotional regulation, and that part of the brain is often called the "affective division" of the cingulate cortex.

Why do humans have these pleasure centers in the brain? Experts theorize that because human survival depends on achieving basic goals such as finding food and procreating, a rush of pleasurable sensations associated with eating or having sex would positively reinforce these behaviors, leading us to repeat them and hence increase the chances that we will survive and reproduce.

Brain and Body Chemistry

Our body chemistry and most particularly our brain chemistry can have a profound effect on our happiness. While our mental states can easily trigger our bodies to react consciously and unconsciously to stress (real or imagined), our moods can also be caused and influenced by our physiology.

If you are sick or tired, run down or recovering from an illness, you will often feel irritated or depressed. Your sense of well-being can be compromised for weeks and sometimes months at a time.

We know that one causal factor of depression is low seratonin levels in the brain, which can be caused by external circumstances, internal beliefs, or even simply a deficit of this vital component of our chemistry.

Even a simple cold or recovering from one can cause a drop in mood for days at a time. Lack of sleep, poor diet and lack of exercise can also be major causes of unhappiness.

The biggest step toward achieving well-being and happiness is to first determine if you are predisposed to "chemical depression," that is, a genetic lack of seratonin levels in the brain.

Even those who eat correctly, exercise regularly and get lots of rest can still suffer the dehabilitating effects of depression if seratonin levels are not sufficient.

If your family has a history of depression and/or you feel down and depressed for long periods of time, you may wish to consult a physician to determine if you are a candidate for anti-depression medication.

Chemical depression is a genetic disorder passed down from generation to generation.

There are many medications available for different types of depression, and sometimes it takes trial and error to determine the type and dosage of medication that works for you, but I can tell you from personal experience that the results can be dramatic.

Alcohol and Drugs

Alcohol and drug abuse is common causes of unhappiness and often go hand in hand with depression. Alcohol is classified as a depressant and will cause depression and sickness of the mind and body.

Avoid alcohol and illicit drugs if you wish to achieve happiness.

Whatever temporary relief from pain and suffering you may derive from these substances and chemicals will be offset and eclipsed by the after-effects, dependency and misery they cause.

Smoking also causes physiological problems that can lead to depression. If you smoke, quit.

Natural balance of mind, body and spirit is the only way to achieve happiness - there are no shortcuts.

How Food Influences Mood

In order for your brain to communicate with your body, it needs chemicals called neurotransmitters to conduct electrical impulses, or brain waves. You may have heard of certain neurotransmitters, such as dopamine, endorphins, glutamine and serotonin. Your body has to manufacture these chemicals and it uses the enzymes, amino acids, minerals, fatty acids, amino acids, proteins and carbohydrates in the foods that you eat to do that. If you're not eating enough - or enough of the right foods - for your body to manufacture sufficient amounts of these chemicals, depression or anxiety can be the result.

Another diet mistake that will lead to low moods is allowing your blood sugar, or glycemic index, to rise and fall throughout the day. Skipping meals can make your blood sugar fall too low, while eating starchy, sugary foods, or simple carbohydrates, such as white bread and pastries, can make your blood sugar too high. This can do funny things to a person's mood, making them irritable, forgetful or sad.

Craving carbohydrates may also be an attempt to self-medicate depression by raising serotonin levels. Serotonin is the neurotransmitter responsible for sleep, appetite and mood.

Eating for Mental Well-Being

Nutrition is central to your mental well-being. Here are some quick tips for keeping your diet in line with your mental health:

•In order to keep your blood sugar steady, eat small meals and healthy snacks throughout the day. Don't skip meals, especially breakfast. Skipping breakfast will likely mean you're still hungry at the end of the day, when you should stop eating in order to prepare for sleep.

- Don't follow any extreme low fat diets. You need some fat to keep your brain working and your mood up. Make sure your diet plan includes healthy, monounsaturated fats, such as those found in olive oil and fatty fish, instead of saturated fats, like the kind found in butter and fast foods.

- Make fresh fruits and vegetables a central part of a healthy diet. Getting enough vitamin B6, folic acid, vitamin C and zinc is essential for your body to manufacture serotonin.

- If you're feeling low, try eating a meal with a food containing the amino acid tryptophan, such as chicken or turkey breast, or milk. Add a carb to your meal, such as a whole grain roll, to help your body absorb the tryptophan more efficiently.

- Limit your consumption of coffee and other caffeinated beverages.

- Don't follow any diet where you cut out an entire food group, such as the Atkins diet.

- Get at least 20 minutes of exercise daily. Exercise helps reduce the severity of anxiety disorder symptoms, such as anxiety attacks.

Comfort Foods

Have you ever noticed how certain smells can make you remember events from your past? Maybe every time you smell a roasting turkey you're eight years old and back in your grandmother's kitchen, or a certain perfume will remind you of an old friend. Well, your senses of taste and smell are tied together too - try eating different foods with your nose plugged sometime, it's just not the same. Eating certain foods is comforting to us because they're tied to happy memories.

Common comfort foods are food commonly associated with childhood; macaroni and cheese, or chocolate cake. These foods also tend to be starchy, and sometimes high in sugar. While it's generally recommended that you try to avoid these types of foods, if you find yourself craving them, it's better to indulge, but with moderation. Trying to ignore your craving will usually lead to binging later on.

Sleeping and Dreaming

The importance of sleep
We all take sleep for granted until we have problems with it and then we quickly remember how desirable a good night's sleep is. Researchers have found a direct link between sleeping and happiness.

The need to sleep is a fundamental human given and it is important for teachers, psychotherapists, employers and others to know something about it if they are to be effective. This is because all human abilities (like paying attention, memory recall and learning) are made worse by poor sleep and there is an intimate relationship between sleep and many psychological conditions — for example, depression, anxiety and psychosis.

Whenever people seem to be having difficulties in their life always enquire about their sleep patterns.

The puzzle of sleeping
It can seem surprising that human beings, who can be so full of life, energy, plans and activities, can, at a certain point each day, disengage from life, lie down and apparently become oblivious to the outside world for up to eight hours. (We spend up to one-third of our life asleep.) When we sleep we are vulnerable to attack since we are no longer aware of what is going on and are in no position to defend ourselves. Yet all mammals, birds and even cold-blooded reptiles sleep so there must be good reasons for it.

Why do we need sleep?

Sleep scientists are increasingly discovering more about this mysterious state. There are two very distinct kinds of sleep: REM (rapid eye movement sleep when we dream) and non-REM sleep, also called slow wave sleep (SWS). During REM sleep there is a paralysis of the anti-gravity muscles and the brain's neocortex and emotional centers become highly aroused.

The waking life of animal organisms is a dynamic, destructive time because the organisms' complex proteins are torn down and exhausted as they are used for activities including locating and ingesting preformed organic molecules to meet the immediate energy needs of the wakened state and to provide the building block proteins which fuel the repair and growth dynamics that occur during sleep.

Slow wave sleep is the dynamic, constructive time of physical healing and growth for animal organisms, a recuperative stage where the mind/body system rebuilds itself after a hard day surviving in the world. Substances ingested during the awake period are synthesized into the complex proteins of living tissue; growth hormones are secreted to assist with the healing of muscles and repairing general wear and tear in tissues; glial cells (neurones in the brain) are refreshed with sugars to restore the brain with energy; the immune system is boosted.

By contrast, in REM sleep large amounts of the brain's energy reserves are expending on dreaming. Dreaming is clearly performing a very important function. Brain wave patterns measured by an electroence-phalogram (EEG) during sleep are similar to waking brain wave patterns. REM sleep occupies about twenty-five percent of a healthy adult's sleep time and dreaming in this state is the deepest trance state known. In the neonate and the foetus REM sleep is the dominant form of sleep and is in some way connected to the programming of instincts into us.

Non-REM sleep is characterized by a slow wave pattern on the EEG. It is divided into stages 1—4 that show an increasingly slow wave pattern, and represent an increasing depth of sleep. In healthy people this sleep pattern lasts about ninety minutes and is followed by REM sleep. Longer periods of REM sleep tend to occur towards the morning.

Sleep problems

In elderly people, REM sleep decreases to about twenty per cent of sleep time and the time spent in deep sleep shortens. They also wake up more frequently. Elderly people often catnap during the day because they don't get such good quality sleep during the night; however, they still require the same amount of sleep. Elderly people are more likely to suffer from insomnia because of an increased likelihood of medical complications. Using too much medication is also a common cause of insomnia, especially in the elderly.

Sleep problems affect every age group. With the rapid change in modern living they are taking an increasing toll on our mental and physical health. Seventeen per cent of the population now has a serious insomnia problem. For millions more people the body's need to have an appropriate amount of quality sleep is frequently compromised to meet their perceived need to have more 'awake' time. If they knew the likely price, they would give an adequate night's sleep a much higher priority.

Sleep is much more than time out from busy schedules; it is essential to the maintenance of physical and psychological health.

Sleep and healing

We sleep more when we are sick with an infection or develop a fever. When our temperature rises, our organs work more quickly, antibodies are synthesized more rapidly and antibiotics are taken up more quickly. It seems that the high temperature may kill off certain microbes.

Even when we are asleep without a fever, our immune function works harder than when we are awake. This explains why many groups of people who are prone to sleep deprivation — junior doctors and other shift workers, for example — suffer more illness and infection than the general population. And why people suffering depression and stress because of the death of a partner are more prone to serious ill-health and more likely than others to die within a year of their spouse's death.

Sleep and accidents
The emotional levels of sleep are also important; the National Sleep Foundation in the USA reports that people with chronic insomnia are more likely than others to develop several kinds of psychiatric problems.

Even temporary sleep loss can impair our ability to concentrate, cope with minor irritations and accomplish tasks, all of which can put a strain on our relationships. When we lose sleep we — and those around us — are at high risk from accidents at work and on the road. For example, a report prepared for the National Commission on Sleep Disorders in the USA arrived at the conservative estimate that sleepiness accounted for nearly forty-two per cent of road accidents. In 1988, a total of 269,184 accidents and 17,687 deaths on the road were caused by sleepy drivers.

The medical profession, of course, also suffers from the effects of sleepiness. The amount of sleep a doctor has is a major factor in his or her ability to detect heart abnormalities. One study showed that rested doctors were fourteen per cent more likely to detect breaks in the normal heart rhythms than were doctors with a sleep deficit. In yet another study sleep-deprived doctors were shown to be extremely indecisive, and videotapes showed that sleep-deprived surgeons operate inefficiently and incompetently for nearly a third of the time.

Perhaps it is not so surprising, then, that research shows that many accidents, mistakes and bad decisions so often caused by people who have too little sleep.

Rest and Relaxation

Life is busy and it seems each year it just gets busier. Work, family, school, and other commitments just eat the day away and leave you with no time to sit back and relax. However, rest and relaxation is very important. In fact, getting enough rest is imperative to living a healthy lifestyle and when you do not relax and get enough sleep you are putting yourself at risk for illness as well as other side effects.

Side Effects of Not Getting Enough Rest

Believe it or not but the body needs enough rest each night to function properly. The amount of rest each individual needs every night differs, however the average adult needs approximately 7-8 hours of sleep each night to restore their body with the energy it needs to handle all of the demands of living each day.

However, most individuals cut back on their sleep to pack more activities into their day. Unfortunately, this runs the body down allowing more viruses and diseases to attack the body because the immune system is not functioning as well as it should. Then, the individual gets sick and misses days or even weeks of all of those important activities. When you get enough rest your body runs as it should and your immune system is stronger and able to fight off infections more easily.

When you don't get enough rest you have difficult concentrating, thinking clearly, and even remembering things. You might not notice this at first or blame it on your busy schedule, but the more sleep you miss and rest you miss out on the more pronounced this symptoms will become.

In addition, a lack of rest and relaxation can really work a number on your mood. It is a scientific fact that when individuals miss out on good nightly rest their personality is affected and they are generally more grumpy, less patient, and snap easier. As a result, missing out on rest to fit in all those activities might make you a bear to be around, which is not much fun at all.

So, the next time you think it is a good idea to stay up late to complete a task or hang out with friends, think again. Of course, one night is not going to hurt you, but night after night of not getting enough rest really will.

Since we are trying to achieve the balance required for happiness, remember to get plenty of rest and relaxation - they are essential to keeping your mood elevated.

Mind Awareness: Mental Aspects of Happiness

Being aware of the mind is the first step toward achieving inner peace and happiness. This is the goal of many forms of meditation, to be able to step outside the mind, to place ones awareness separately from the chatter of the mind and to become a casual observer.

Our conscious and unconscious thoughts are a constant stream of negative chatter, keeping us in a constant state of dissonance and worry.

Even if we seem to be calm on the surface and go through our day with what appears to be a sense of normalcy and functional coping, below the surface of our awareness our unconscious thoughts run in the background, a low level hum of discontent, like static on a frequency we cannot hear but it's there just the same.

But the mind's natural, pure state is the mind level we wish to achieve.

Pure Mind - Perfect Mind

The mind's pure natural state is one that is in harmony with the universe, puts us in perfect balance, and allows us to be in the moment and to experience happiness in its most joyous form.

It is a state of mind in which one is not affected by the dual concepts of good and bad.

In its natural state, the mind is the same - in it, there exists no loving or hating, nor does it seek to blame other people. It is independent, existing in a state of purity that is truly clear, radiant and untarnished.

In its pure state, the mind is peaceful, without happiness or suffering - indeed, not experiencing any feeling at all. This is the true state of the mind. The purpose of the practice of meditation or mindfulness , then, is to seek inwardly, searching and investigating until you reach the original mind.

The original mind is also known as the pure mind. The pure mind is the mind without attachment. It doesn't get affected by mind-objects. In other words, it doesn't chase after the different kinds of pleasant and unpleasant mind-objects. Rather, the mind is in a state of continuous knowing and wakefulness - thoroughly mindful of all it is experiencing. When the mind is like this, no pleasant or unpleasant mind-objects it experiences will be able to disturb it. The mind doesn't 'become' anything. In other words, nothing can shake it. The mind knows itself as pure. It has evolved its own, true independence; it has reached its original state.

How is it able to bring this original state into existence?

Through the faculty of mindfulness wisely reflecting and seeing that all things are merely conditions arising out of the influence of elements, without any individual being controlling them. This is how it is with the happiness and suffering we experience.

When these mental states arise, they are just 'happiness' and 'suffering'. There is no owner of the happiness. The mind is not the owner of the suffering - mental states do not belong to the mind. Look at it for yourself.

In reality these are not affairs of the mind, they are separate and distinct. Happiness is just the state of happiness; suffering is just the state of suffering. You are merely the knower of these.

In the past, because the roots of greed, hatred and delusion already existed in the mind, whenever you caught sight of the slightest pleasant or unpleasant mind-object, the mind would react immediately - you would take hold of it and have to experience either happiness or suffering.

You would be continuously indulging in states of happiness and suffering. That's the way it is as long as the mind doesn't know itself - as long as it's not bright and illuminated The mind is not free. It is influenced by whatever mind-objects it experiences.

In other words, it is without a refuge, unable to truly depend on itself. You receive a pleasant mental impression and get into a good mood.

The mind forgets itself.

Accept and Allow
When negative thoughts and emotions occur as a result of circumstances that happen in your life that you don't agree with, simply learn to detach; accept and allow.

You cannot change the things that inevitably happen in your life that are beyond your control.

Consciousness, Awareness and Being
Watch closely your consciousness, this feeling and sensation of being aware and alive, and observe what you feel. I do not mean

that you look at the contents of your mind. I mean becoming fully aware and conscious of the sensation of being alive and existing. Some concentration ability is required to perform this simple exercise, because the mind and its thoughts will probably try to stand in your way.

This consciousness I am referring to, is not the awareness of having a body, emotions or thoughts, but of something beyond.

This consciousness is your inner being, and there is nothing mysterious or mystical about it. We all experience this consciousness constantly, but never investigate or try to be consciously and intently aware of it. This is because the mind and the attention flow outside, and rarely inside.

You might ask: "Why do I need to be aware of this consciousness? I have never thought about it before. Why now?"

You are this consciousness - it is your being, and you therefore need to know about it. If you own a car, don't you want to know, at least superficially, how to take care of it? If you own a TV, a mobile phone or some other electrical appliance, don't you want to know how to use it efficiently, and understand, at least a little, how it works?

The more you become aware of your consciousness, the more you become conscious and aware of its power, and can utilize its power. Calmness, peace of mind, freedom from anxiety and worry, inner strength and happiness are some of the by-products of becoming conscious and aware of your inner consciousness.

When watching a beautiful, breathtaking landscape, do you sometimes become immersed and overwhelmed by it, and for some moments you cease to be aware of your body, feelings and thoughts? For a little while you become merged in some sort of silence.

A little while later, your mind starts verbalizing about the landscape, and you become aware again of your feelings and thoughts. You return to your ordinary consciousness and awareness of your body and its sensations.

You did not lose consciousness during this experience. It was a happy and joyous experience, in which you became aware of something beyond your ordinary awareness.

This consciousness is beyond the body, feelings and thoughts. It is beyond beliefs, attitudes, names, gender, family and social or economic status. It is your inner being.

Body feelings and thoughts are changeable and impermanent. Even the cells of the body change in time. Yet, the Higher Consciousness never changes. It is immutable. It holds everything else together like a string that holds a necklace of pearls. It is constant, but all the "things" attached to it or revolving around it always change.

When you reject every component as not your "I", the residue that remains is something, which cannot be described, only lived. It is an impersonal "I". It cannot be the object of thought, because it is above and beyond thoughts and the mind.

You can know, experience and be this "I", but you cannot think about it or analyze it, as it is not an outside object. This "I", this consciousness is the real you.

Discussing this consciousness is just mental acrobatics, because this consciousness is beyond thoughts. It is fully experienced only when thoughts cease, whether unintentionally, as in the above case of watching a landscape, or intentionally when special exercises are performed to enhance it.

By teaching yourself to be aware and immersed of this consciousness, the mind and the flow of thoughts calm down, and you experience inner peace. This is usually done through meditation and proper mental attitude.

Being able to concentrate is a great help. Reading spiritual literature, or coming in contact with people who are living in constant spiritual awareness are great aids. Your practice should be done in a relaxed and calm way, without thinking of the target or worrying about it too much.

You do not need to search for this Consciousness. It is here, and you are living in it all the time. You only forgot it. You are letting thoughts rule your life. The sky is always up there. If you don't see it, this is because of the clouds that cover it. In the same way the clouds of thoughts cover your Consciousness, but by removing them you become aware of it.

This Consciousness I am talking about, is not the everyday, ordinary awareness of our body, ego and personality. It is not the awareness of the world around us. It is a sort of "Higher Consciousness" that stands beyond the ordinary one, and is responsible for it.

The ordinary consciousness is changeable and intermittent. At times we are aware of the outer world and at other times unaware or only partially aware. There are times of sleep and times of wakefulness. Yet, the "Inner Consciousness" is always present. It never ceases to be and is always present. It is at the background of whatever happens in life.

Developing the power of concentration, practicing meditation and trying to be aware of your Awareness, Consciousness, and Being, is the way to the golden key that opens the door of Enlightenment.

Sense Pleasure Happiness (and Why It Doesn't Last)

This refers to enjoyment of sensory pleasures – food, aromas, music, roller coasters, sex, hot showers... the kinds of things that make you go, "Ahh.. ."

But before you say to yourself, "That's my kind of evening," keep in mind that pleasures get old fast. You may have noticed, for example, that the first bite of chocolate mousse tastes the best; the eighth bite is just calories. That's because of the brain's tendency to adapt and to progressively ignore repeated sensory input.

Here's what Martin Seligman recommends to help you enjoy the pleasures over time:

• **Savor the moment. Share it with others. Pay attention and sharpen your perception. Take a mental picture.**

• **Be mindful of the context of your experience. Practice meditation
techniques to increase your mindfulness.**

• **Space your pleasures. This will counteract the effects of habituation that reduces pleasure.**

While pleasures feel good, they don't last. And pursuing one sensual indulgence after another eventually feels empty, devoid of purpose and meaning.

A much more enduring path to happiness is the engaged life, which usually involves a task, a project or an activity, as well as an intellectual or physical challenge.

The "If Only" Delusion

Often our minds tell us that "if only" a certain condition or situation existed (or didn't exist) we could then be happy. What many of us fail to realize is that we already have everything we need to be happy, if we could simply get rid of unrealistic expectations and desires!

Understand that no situation needs to exist or not exist for you to experience true happiness now. If you are feeling unhappy, know that it is in your mind where the unhappiness exists.

This is tough concept to grasp when we have been telling ourselves our entire lives that a certain thing needs to happen to cease to happen for us to be happy.

Advertising and the media feed on this delusion by convincing us that if we buy their product we will be happy. But know that no matter what you buy, that if you are not happy deep within yourself before you bought it, then no purchase or acquisition will bring lasting solace.

Everything You Need To Be Happy You Already Possess

Dr. Wayne Dyer, the popular author and lecturer on self-actualization, has good things to tell us about what all of us already has within us.

"Our ego tells us who we should be, how we should live, and the definition of success and happiness; which is a lie because it's all based on external sources. The truth is that everything we need to be happy and fulfilled is already inside of us, given to use by our creator."

"The same force that gave us everything we needed in the womb is still with us; thus we still have access to anything we need to live our life on purpose. We just need to get our ego out of the way, be open minded and willing, and let the universe bring it to us. However, we must not confuse this idea with procrastination; we must take action to prepare ourselves in being ready and able to recognize these moments and gifts as they arrive. Anything else is still primarily our ego talking."

"If everything we need to become who we are is already in us, why do we continually seek outside of ourselves for happiness and purpose? Because we're still living for and by ego; telling us if only we had this or that we'd be happy."

"We all have an inner voice telling us there must be something more out there, some purpose to our lives. Start listening to it! Think about how you lean in to overhear a conversation that catches your interest. Maybe you're thinking these people are weak or you're too proud to ask them questions, but you still sort of lean in and want to know more. Start listening to that need to know and want more out of life and let it take you to where you're destined to go."

Money and Happiness (They Aren't Related)

It's official: Money can't buy happiness.

Sure, if a person is handed $10, the pleasure centers of his brain light up as if he were given food, sex or drugs. But that initial rush does not translate into long-term pleasure for most people. Surveys have found virtually the same level of happiness between the very rich individuals on the Forbes 400 and the Maasai herdsman of East Africa. Lottery winners return to their previous level of happiness after five years. Increases in income just don't seem to make people happier--and most negative life experiences likewise have only a small impact on long-term satisfaction.

"The relationship between money and happiness is pretty darned small," says Peter Ubel, a professor of medicine at the University of Michigan.

That's not to say that increased income doesn't matter at all. There is a very small correlation between wealth and happiness-- accounting for about 1% of the happiness reported by people answering surveys. And for some groups, that relationship may be considerably bigger. People who are poor seem to get much happier when their monetary prospects improve, as do the very sick. In these cases, Ubel speculates, people may be protected from negative circumstances by the extra cash. Another possibility is that the money brings an increase in status, which may have a greater impact on happiness.

Why doesn't wealth bring a constant sense of joy? "Part of the reason is that people aren't very good at figuring out what to do with the money," says George Loewenstein, an economist at Carnegie Mellon University. People generally overestimate the amount of long-term pleasure they'll get from a given object.

Sometimes, Loewenstein notes, the way people spend their money can actually make them less happy. For example, people derive a great deal of pleasure from interacting with others. If the first thing lottery winners do is quit their job and move to a palatial but isolated estate where they don't see any neighbors, they could find themselves isolated and depressed.

Other trophies simply don't bring the payoff one expects. Says Loewenstein, "If you're a single male driving around in the Ferrari with nobody next to you, it's a glaring omission."

The central problem is that the human brain becomes conditioned to positive experiences. Getting a chunk of unexpected money registers as a good thing, but as time passes, the response wears off. An expected paycheck doesn't bring any buzz at all--and doesn't contribute to overall happiness. You can get used to anything, be it hanging by your toenails or making millions of dollars a day. Mood may be set more by heredity than by anything else: Studies of twins have shown that at least half a person's level of happiness may be determined by some of the genes that play a role in determining personality.

But this raises another question. How important is happiness anyway? People with chronic illnesses describe themselves as happy, but they would still pay large sums for better health. And although healthy individuals are not much happier than quadriplegics, they would pay large sums of money to keep the use of their limbs. Some of life's most satisfying experiences don't bring happiness. For instance, having children actually makes people less happy over the short term--but that doesn't necessarily mean we should stop procreating.

"I think it's possible to way overestimate the importance of happiness," says Loewenstein. "Part of the meaning of life is to have highs and lows. A life that was constantly happy was not a good life."

However, there may be at least one important relationship between money and happiness, according to Ed Diener, the University of Illinois researcher who surveyed the Forbes 400 and the Maasai. Diener has also written that happy people tend to have higher incomes later on in their lives. So, while money may not help make people happy, being happy may help them make money.

Stress Factors

What is Stress
We generally use the word "stress" when we feel that everything seems to have become too much - we are overloaded and wonder whether we really can cope with the pressures placed upon us.

Anything that poses a challenge or a threat to our well-being is a stress. Some stresses get you going and they are good for you - without any stress at all many say our lives would be boring and would probably feel pointless. However, when the stresses undermine both our mental and physical health they are bad. In this text we shall be focusing on stress that is bad for you.

Fight or flight response

The way you respond to a challenge may also be a type of stress. Part of your response to a challenge is physiological and affects your physical state. When faced with a challenge or a threat, your body activates resources to protect you - to either get away as fast as you can, or fight.

If you are upstairs at home and an earthquake starts, the faster you can get yourself and your family out the more likely you are all to survive. If you need to save somebody's life during that earthquake, by lifting a heavy weight that has fallen on them during the earthquake, you will need components in your body to be activated to give you that extra strength - that extra push.

Our fight-or-flight response is our body's sympathetic nervous system reacting to a stressful event. Our body produces larger quantities of the chemicals cortisol, adrenaline and noradrenaline, which trigger a higher heart rate, heightened muscle preparedness, sweating, and alertness - all these factors help us protect ourselves in a dangerous or challenging situation.

Non-essential body functions slow down, such as our digestive and immune systems when we are in fight-or flight response mode. All resources can then be concentrated on rapid breathing, blood flow, alertness and muscle use.

So, let's recap, when we are stressed the following happens:

-Blood pressure rises
-Breathing becomes more rapid
-Digestive system slows down

-Heart rate (pulse) rises
-Immune system goes down
-Muscles become tense
-We do not sleep (heightened state of alertness)

Most of us have varying interpretations of what stress is about and what matters. Some of us focus on what happens to us, such as breaking a bone or getting a promotion, while others think more about the event itself. What really matters are our thoughts about the situations in which we find ourselves.

We are continually sizing up situations that confront us in life. We assess each situation, deciding whether something is a threat, how we can deal with it and what resources we can use.

If we conclude that the required resources needed to effectively deal with a situation are beyond what we have available, we say that that situation is stressful - and we react with a classical stress response. On the other hand, if we decide our available resources and skills are more than enough to deal with a situation, it is not seen as stressful to us.

We all respond differently to a given situation for three main reasons

1. We do not all interpret each situation in the same way.
2. Because of this, we do not all call on the same resources for each situation
3. We do not all have the same resources and skills.

Some situations which are not negative ones may still be perceived as stressful. This is because we think we are not completely prepared to cope with them effectively. Examples being: having a baby, moving to a nicer house, and being promoted. Having a baby is usually a wonderful thing, so is being promoted or moving to a nicer house. But, moving house is a well-known source of stress.

It is important to learn that what matters more than the event itself is usually our thoughts about the event when we are trying to manage stress. How you see that stressful event will be the largest single factor that impacts on your physical and mental health. Your interpretation of events and challenges in life may decide whether they are invigorating or harmful for you.

A persistently negative response to challenges will eventually have a negative effect on your health and happiness. Experts say people who tend to perceive things negatively need to understand themselves and their reactions to stress-provoking situations better. Then they can learn to manage stress more successfully.

Some of the effects of stress on your body, your thoughts and feelings, and on your behavior:

Effect on your body
A tendency to sweat
Back pain
Chest pain
Cramps or muscle spasms
Erectile dysfunction
Fainting spells
Headache
Heart disease
Hypertension (high blood pressure)
Loss of libido
Lower immunity against diseases
Muscular aches
Nail biting
Nervous twitches
Pins and needles
Sleeping difficulties
Stomach upset

Effect on your thoughts and feelings
Anger
Anxiety
Burnout
Depression
Feeling of insecurity
Forgetfulness
Irritability
Problem concentrating
Restlessness
Sadness
Fatigue

Effect on your behavior
Eating too much
Eating too little
Food cravings
Sudden angry outbursts
Drug abuse
Alcohol abuse
Higher tobacco consumption
Social withdrawal
Frequent crying
Relationship problems

What are the causes of stress?
We all react differently to stressful situations. What one person finds stressful another may not at all. Almost anything can cause stress and it has different triggers. For some people, on some occasions, just thinking about something, or several small things that accumulate, can cause stress.

The most common causes of stress are:
Bereavement
Family problems
Financial matters
Illness
Job issues

Lack of time
Moving home
Relationships (including divorce)
The following are also causes of stress
Abortion
Becoming a mother or a father
Conflicts in the workplace
Driving in bad traffic
Fear of crime
Losing your job
Miscarriage
Noisy neighbors
Overcrowding
Pollution
Pregnancy
Retirement
Too much noise
Uncertainty (awaiting laboratory test results, academic exam results, job interview results, etc)

It is possible that a person feels stressed and no clear cause is identified. A feeling of frustration, anxiety and depression can make some people feel stressed more easily than others.

Diagnosis of stress

A good primary care physician (GP - General Practitioner) should be able to diagnose stress based on the patient's symptoms alone. Some doctors may wish to run some tests, such as a blood or urine, or a health assessment.

The diagnosis of stress depends on many factors and is complex, say experts. A wide range of approaches to stress diagnosis have been used by health care professionals, such as the use of questionnaires, biochemical measures, and physiological techniques. Experts add that the majority of these methods are subject to experimental error and should be viewed with caution. The most practicable way to diagnose stress and its effects on a person is through a comprehensive, stress-oriented, face-to-face interview.

How to deal with stress
There are three broad methods you can follow to treat stress, they include self-help, self management, and medication.

Self help for treating stress
Exercise - exercise has been proven to have a beneficial effect on a person's mental and physical state. For many people exercise is an extremely effective stress buster.

Division of labor - try to delegate your responsibilities at work, or share them. If you make yourself indispensable the likelihood of your feeling highly stressed is significantly greater.

Assertiveness - don't say yes to everything. If you can't do something well, or if something is not your responsibility, try to seek ways of not agreeing to do them.

Alcohol and drugs - alcohol and drugs will not help you manage your stress better. Either stop consuming them completely, or cut down.

Caffeine - if your consumption of coffee and other drinks which contain caffeine is high, cut down.

Nutrition - eat plenty of fruit and vegetables. Make sure you have a healthy and balanced diet.

Time - make sure you set aside some time each day just for yourself. Use that time to organize your life, relax, and pursue your own interests.

Breathing - there are some effective breathing techniques which will slow down your system and help you relax.

Talk - talk to you family, friends, work colleagues and your boss. Express your thoughts and worries.

Seek professional help - if the stress is affecting the way you function; go and see your doctor. Heightened stress for prolonged periods can be bad for your physical and mental health.

Relaxation techniques - mediation, massage, or yoga have been known to greatly help people with stress.

Stress management techniques

Stress management can help you to either remove or change the source of stress, alter the way you view a stressful event, lower the impact that stress might have on your body, and teach you alternative ways of coping. Stress management therapy will have the objective of pursuing one or more of these approaches.

Stress management techniques can be gained if you read self-help books, or attend a stress management course. You can also seek the help of a counselor or psychotherapist for personal development or therapy sessions.

Many therapies which help you relax, such as aromatherapy, or reflexology, may have a beneficial effect.

Stress In The Animal Kingdom

Studies of baboons in the animal kingdom have shown remarkable similarities between the stresses they experience and our own lives.

Biologist Robert M. Sapolsky of Stanford University explored some of his findings in his book *Why Zebras Don't Get Ulcers.* (2004) The book proclaims itself as a "Guide to Stress, Stress-Related Diseases, and Coping" on the front cover of its third and most recent edition.

The name stems from Sapolsky's insistence that wild animals are less susceptible than humans to stress-related disorders such as ulcers, hypertension, decreased neurogenesis and increased hippocampal neuronal atrophy.

Sapolsky focuses on the effects of glucocorticoids on the human body, stating that such hormones may be useful to animals in the wild escaping their predators, but the effects on humans, when secreted at high quantities or over long periods of time, are much less desired.

Sapolsky relates the history of endocrinology, how the field reacted at times of discovery, and how it has changed through the years. While most of the book focuses on the biological machinery of the body, the last chapter of the book focuses on self-help.

Noise Pollution

What Is Noise Pollution?
Noise pollution can be defined as intrusive noise that disrupts, distracts, or detracts from regular functioning. And while people mainly think of noise pollution as a problem of the big cities, with the competing sounds of more people in a smaller space, noise pollution can also be found in suburban neighborhoods (in the form of leaf blowers, lawn mowers, and home construction) and even individual homes and offices at levels that can have a negative impact on your health and productivity.

It can definitely put a damper on your pursuit of happiness, peace and contentment!

Causes of Noise Pollution
While there are many different sources of noise pollution, there are some main culprits that have been researched and found to have a negative impact on health. They include the following:

•**Airplanes**: It's been well-documented that noise pollution from airplanes has a significant negative impact on the health and wellbeing of those who live close to airports. This can include heart disease, high blood pressure and chronic stress. (About.com's Environment Guide has more information on the effects of airports and noise pollution.)

•**Cars**: One of the complaints of those who live in big cities or on busy streets is the disruption from the sounds of traffic. Interestingly, though, even low levels of traffic noise can be damaging to people, and traffic noise is one of the most commonly experienced contributors to noise pollution.

•**Workplace Noise**: Most of us may think of loud assembly lines or construction sites when we think of noise pollution in the workplace, and while these examples definitely apply, regular offices are not immune. With more people packed into busy office spaces, office noise is a common complaint. Co-workers who talk, drum their fingers on the desk, or offer other distracting noises can decrease the productivity of those around them without realizing it.

•Home Sound--Many people don't think of their homes as 'noisy', but if there's a lot of activity in the home, including a constantly running t.v., this overall noise level can actually be a threat to concentration and a cause of stress. In fact, children from more noisy homes do suffer ill effects from this type of sound pollution that include less cognitive growth, delayed language skills, increased anxiety, and impaired resilience, according to a Purdue University professor in a related press release.

Negative Effects of Noise Pollution

Many studies have been conducted to study the effects of noise pollution on health and wellness, and the results have shown that noise pollution can negatively impact you in the following ways:

•**Productivity**: We all know that noise can be distracting, and research proves this. One study examined children exposed to airport noise and found that their reading ability and long-term memory was impaired. Those working in noisy office environments have also been found to be less cognitively motivated, and to have higher stress levels, according to a Cornell University study.

•**Health:** Perhaps the most serious problem created by sound pollution is the impact it has on our health. Because sound pollution can trigger the body's stress response, one of its major health effects is chronic stress and the high levels of stress hormones that go with it. As a result, noise pollution has also been linked with health problems such as heart disease, high blood pressure, and stroke. It's also been linked with musculoskeletal problems, as a Cornell University study on office noise found that those working in noisy office environments can also be less likely to ergonomically adjust their workstations for comfort, which can contribute to physical problems. Noise pollution can also impact sleep quality by preventing sleep and disrupting sleep cycles. And, perhaps most significantly, because chronic stress can lower your immunity to all disease, noise pollution is a general threat to health and wellness.

Eliminating Noise Pollution
noise pollution can negatively impact the body in significant ways, including elevated blood pressure, impaired cognitive functioning, and other effects of chronic stress. (This article explains it in more detail.) The following are effective strategies you can use to limit the negative impact of noise pollution and safeguard your health and happiness.

Limit The Noise
Your first line of defense against noise pollution is to do what you can to control your environment, and limit the noise that enters your space. The following are ways that you can limit environmental noise and blunt the effects of noise pollution:

•**Double-Paned Windows and Weather Stripping:** If you live in a noisy city or near an airport, you can reduce noise in your home considerably by installing dual-paned windows, weather stripping, and even added insulation. As a bonus, these changes can also reduce your heating and cooling bills, and help the environment!

•**Reduce Workplace Noise:** If you work in a noisy office, you may want to talk to your employer about taking steps to reduce office noise, which has been found to affect the health and productivity of workers.
•**Turn Off The T.V.:** When you're at home, a constant backdrop of television can have an effect on you as a distraction and potential stressor.

•**Make Bigger Changes:** You may even consider moving or changing jobs if you experience significant levels of noise that you can't reduce in other ways. It sounds like a drastic step, but considering the toll that a noisy environment can take on your health, it may be an option to consider.

If you can't eliminate noise from your environment, you can actually create a healthier environment by replacing stress-inducing environmental sounds with more pleasing ones. For example, you can reduce the impact of airport or city noise with a white noise machine or 'sound spa'. They play sounds ranging from waterfalls to rain to babbling brooks to basic static, and these sounds mask the more jarring environmental noises that can distract you or negatively affect your sleep. They can also make it easier to meditate or practice visualization techniques.

Additionally, you can drown out distracting sounds from a noisy office environment or neighborhood with music from your iPod or stereo and enjoy the stress management and health benefits of music while lessening the impact of the other noise. This can also improve your mood, boost your immunity, calm your physiology, or energize you. While you're really trading some sounds for others, the sounds of nature or music can be more soothing and better for your health.

Because part of the toll of noise pollution is due to the activation of the body's stress response, it stands to reason that you can counteract some of these ill effects by regularly using techniques that can reverse your body's physiological changes that come with chronic stress. The following are some of the most effective techniques you can use:

•Breathing Exercises: Deep breathing and other breathing exercises work well because they can be done anywhere and are effective in calming the body's physiology in minutes. (Take a deep breath...don't you feel better already?)

•**Meditation:** Meditation is also an extremely effective stress reliever because it calms the physiology and even helps alter brain chemistry so that, over time, you are less reactive to stress as it happens. (For more in meditation, read these articles on the benefits of meditation and different types of meditation that can be helpful to you.)

•**Yoga**: The practice of yoga is a great stress reliever because it combines breathing and meditation, and adds an element of exercise to be a stress reliever that acts on several different levels to benefit your health. It also provides a simple way to ease into meditation, for those who find it to be a bit of a challenge at first.

Coping Factors: Stress In The Workplace

Jobs and careers are an important part of our lives. Along with providing a source of income, they help us fulfill our personal aims, build social networks, and serve our professions or communities. They are also a major source of emotional stress.

Stress at work

Even "dream jobs" have stressful deadlines, performance expectations, and other responsibilities. For some, stress is the motivator that ensures things get done. However, workplace stress can easily overwhelm your life. You may continually worry about a particular project, feel unfairly treated by a supervisor or co-workers, or knowingly accept more than you can handle in hopes of earning a promotion. Putting your job ahead of everything else can also affect your personal relationships, compounding the work-related pressures.

Layoffs, restructuring, or management changes can heighten anxiety about your job security. In fact, a Norwegian study showed that the mere rumor of a factory's closure caused rapid increases in workers' pulse and blood pressure. Research in the U.S. has found that workplace injuries and accidents tend to increase in organizations that are being downsized.

The body reacts to stress

Along with its emotional toll, prolonged job-related stress can drastically affect your physical health. Constant preoccupation with job responsibilities often leads to erratic eating habits and not enough exercise, resulting in weight problems, high blood pressure, and elevated cholesterol levels.

Common job stressors such as perceived low rewards, a hostile work environment, and long hours can also accelerate the onset of heart disease, including the likelihood of heart attacks.
This is particularly true for blue-collar and manual workers. Studies suggest that because these employees tend to have little control over their work environments, they are more likely to develop cardiovascular disease than those in traditional "white collar" jobs.

Your age is also a factor. A University of Utah study found that as stressed workers get older, their blood pressure increases above normal levels. Interestingly, many of the study's over-60 workers reported that they did not feel upset or unduly pressured by their jobs, even though their blood pressure levels were significantly higher.

Job stress also frequently causes burnout, a condition marked by emotional exhaustion and negative or cynical attitudes toward others and yourself.

Burnout can lead to depression, which, in turn, has been linked to a variety of other health concerns such as heart disease and stroke, obesity and eating disorders, diabetes, and some forms of cancer. Chronic depression also reduces your immunity to other types of illnesses, and can even contribute to premature death.

What you can do to combat job stress

Fortunately, there are many ways to help manage job-related stress. Some programs blend relaxation techniques with nutrition and exercise. Others focus on specific issues such as time management, assertiveness training, and improving social skills.

A qualified psychologist or other mental health professional can help you pinpoint the causes of your stress, and develop appropriate coping strategies.

Here are some other tips for dealing with stress on the job:

•Make the most of workday breaks.

•Even 10 minutes of "personal time" will refresh your mental outlook. Take a brief walk, chat with a co-worker about a non-job topic, or simply sit quietly with your eyes closed and breathe.

•If you feel angry, walk away. Mentally regroup by counting to 10, then look at the situation again. Walking and other physical activities will also help you work off steam.

•Set reasonable standards for yourself and others. Don't expect perfection.

•Talk to your employer about your job description. Your responsibilities and performance criteria may not accurately reflect what you are doing.

Working together to make needed changes will not only benefit your emotional and physical health, but also improve the organization's overall productivity.

Stress While Driving

Stress while driving can create a lot of roadblocks to your inner peace of mind.

In a study conducted at the University of California at Irvine, researcher s discovered that the stress of commuting takes a big toll on health. According to the research, it has direct physiological causes of increasing blood pressure and releasing stress hormones into the body. Not just that, long commutes (more than 18 miles one way) could also increase the likelihood of having a heart attack because of exposure to high levels of air pollutants, which seems to be a risk factor for heart disease.

Even though there is no antidote to stressful commuting, there are a lot of ways to shoo off this energy vulture. Here's how to thrive while you drive.

1. Prepare in advance

One of the best ways to diminish the strain of road rage is to prepare the whole thing the previous night. Clothes, documents, attached cases, and even filled lunches should be set the day before to stay away from the morning rush. With everything champing at the bit, you'd save plenty of time to do your morning routines, consume a good breakfast and enjoy special moments with the family. Better yet, you can dash out the highway free of traffic congestion.

2. Sleep well and wake up early

A good night's sleep rejuvenates your body. Make it a habit to have enough sleep and to increase soon. If you're already stressed out the day before, an incomplete repose takes over cumulative stress causes into your life at work and at home. Your frustration levels at the work place in the end increases, your brainpower falters, and your mood at home sours. You have no more energy left to enjoy life.

3. Juggle your work hours

Do you really enjoy working the typical 9 to 5 job? Why pack the freeways when you can try a ten-to-six or an eight-to-four shift? Of course, not all companies will allow you to have flexible hours, but at least attempt to check out other available shifts that fit your lifestyle. Choose one that would help you get rid of energy-depleting stress and allow you to lighten your highway woes.

4. Share your ride

It might be a hassle to organize your arrival and departure with another individual or two, but many times carpooling is worth it. Studies show that ridesharing lowers commuter stress significantly. With carpooling, there is less air and noise pollution, less traffic congestion, and you could relax more when someone else is doing the driving.

5. "Cocoon" in your auto

Instead of getting agitated when traffic is at a standstill, try to use your time wisely. Listen to your favorite radio station or pop in some good music CDs to take your mind off the end-and-go driving and traffic tie-ups. If you like to read but just don't have time to flip pages of a book, check out books or audio books. Lots of libraries have full-length audio books in addition to abridged versions. You could even learn a new language or do several car exercises like neck extensions, shoulder rolls and tummy tucks to help you stay awake and relax.

6. Pillow your back and squirm

When you're standing, the lumbar area of your spine (the lower part) generally curves inward, toward your abdomen. However, when you're sitting, it has a tendency to slump outward pressing on your spinal disks and putting stress on them. According to back specialist Malcolm Pope, Ph.D., director of the Iowa Spine Research Center at the University of Iowa, it helps in supporting your back by tucking a rolled towel or a pillow in that lumbar section. In cases of longer drives, because sitting in one position for longer than 15 minutes slowly stiffens you even with a back pillow, make required adjustments for a comfy ride. For example, you can try putting most of your weight on one buttock and then the other. Then, shift the position of your seat or your buttocks somewhat. You might even try sliding down in your seat and sit up again for fun.

7. Take a break

It might be a good thought to offer yourself some day off from work. Many companies nowadays offer compressed working hours or longer working days to provide way to work-free days for you to unwind.

8. Exercise after work

Since the evening hurry is worse than the morning hurry as a result of the compounded fatigue from the workday, it is recommended to wait out the traffic. Work out at a gym near your office or take meditation classes to relieve your driving stress. If you are planning on going to dinner, seeing a movie or going shopping, try to do these things near work, delaying your departure enough to miss the maddening hurry.

9. Move your office

If your job is a long drive ahead daily, inquire at the work place if the company would let you work at home some days of the week or if you could work close your place. With today's technology this could be very possible. An alternative work schedule would make you feel less tense and in charge thereby decreasing stress.

10. Change your routine from time to time

An occasional change of commuting habits might be recommended also. You may also try walking or even bicycling from time to time for a change. There's nothing like a good walk to ease tension, particularly when it means you don't have to get in your car and fight rush hour traffic.

By diminishing the stress of getting to work, you're conserving huge sums of energy that might be lost over commuting stress. It doesn't just leave you much more energy to do your job and become more useful but it also makes you feel good and gives you a good motive to always start your day right.

Dealing With Difficult People and Avoiding Conflict

Research shows that supportive relationships are good for our mental and physical health. However, dealing with difficult people and maintaining ongoing negative relationships is actually detrimental to our health. It's a good idea to diminish or eliminate relationships that are filled with conflict. But what do you do if the person in question is a family member, co-worker, or someone you otherwise can't easily eliminate from your life?

The following are tips for dealing with difficult people who are in your life, for better or for worse:

1. Keep Conversations Neutral:
Avoid discussing divisive and personal issues, like religion and politics, or other issues that tend to cause conflict. If the other person tries to engage you in a discussion that will probably become an argument, change the subject or leave the room.

2. Accept The Reality of Who They:
Are In dealing with difficult people, don't try to change the other person; you will only get into a power struggle, cause defensiveness, invite criticism, or otherwise make things worse. It also makes you a more difficult person to deal with.

3. Know What's Under Your Control:
Change your response to the other person; this is all you have the power to change. For example, don't feel you need to accept abusive behavior. You can use assertive communication to draw boundaries when the other person chooses to treat you in an unacceptable way.

4. Create Healthier Patterns:
Remember that most relationship difficulties are due to a dynamic between two people rather than one person being unilaterally "bad." Chances are good that you're repeating the same patterns of interaction over and over; changing your response could get you out of this rut, and responding in a healthy way can improve your chances of a healthier pattern forming. Here's a list of things to avoid in dealing with conflict. Do you do any of them?

5. See The Best In People:
Try to look for the positive aspects of others, especially when dealing with family, and focus on them. The other person will feel more appreciated, and you will likely enjoy your time together more.

6. Remember Who You're Dealing With:
Seeing the best in someone is important; however, don't pretend the other person's negative traits don't exist. Don't tell your secrets to a gossip, rely on a flake, or look for affection from someone who isn't able to give it. This is part of accepting them for who they are.

7. Get Support Where You Can Find It:
Get your needs met from others who are able to meet your needs. Tell your secrets to a trustworthy friend who's a good listener, or process your feelings through journaling, for example. Rely on people who have proven themselves to be trustworthy and supportive, or find a good therapist if you need one. This will help you and the other person by taking pressure off the relationship and removing a source of conflict.

8. Let Go Or Get Space:
 If You Need It Know when it's time to distance yourself, and do so. If the other person can't be around you without antagonizing you, minimizing contact may be key. If they're continually abusive, it's best to cut ties and let them know why. Explain what needs to happen if there ever is to be a relationship, and let it go. (If the offending party is a boss or co-worker, you may consider switching jobs.)

Tips:
1. Try not to place blame on yourself or the other person for the negative interactions. It may just be a case of your two personalities fitting poorly.

2. Remember that you don't have to be close with everyone; just being polite goes a long way toward getting along and appropriately dealing with difficult people.

3. Work to maintain a sense of humor -- difficulties will roll off your back much more easily. Shows like "The Office" and books

like David Sedaris' Naked can help you see the humor in dealing with difficult people.

4. Be sure to cultivate other more positive relationships in your life to offset the negativity of dealing with difficult people.

Reading - The Beginning Of Liberation

The pursuit of human happiness is a timeless quest. People throughout the ages have sought to be happy, and centuries of writing await us like buried treasure.

There are also many contemporary books on happiness, and include a reading list of recommended titles as the end of this book.

Understanding just what makes happiness in our lives begins with reading, for it's often hard to see the forest for the trees and be objective when we are immersed in our own problems.

Getting outside of ourselves is the first step toward liberation, to separate ourselves from our perceived identity.

Reading can help us to remember things we can't possibly keep in our minds at all times, especially when the ego is fighting for survival.

The Practice of Happiness

Happiness is a choice. Like physical fitness, happiness is something we must work at every day. It's easy to fall into negative thought patterns, simply because it's easier to let our "monkey-mind" run rampant through the jungle!

9 Habits of Happy People

True happiness is priceless. We can't buy it, and no one can hand it to us. It is part of the human experience, and it comes from within us. We can make ourselves happy or unhappy when no one and nothing else can. That is because we control how we think and how we respond to life. Basically, we make choices every day that determine whether or not we're going to enjoy our lives and be our best.

If we want to be happy, we have to do something about it. Developing a lifestyle of happiness requires work and a great deal of practice. The more we practice happiness, the more natural it will become. The problem is, most people, don't know how to practice happiness. We hear about the characteristics of happy people, but we don't know how to make them real in our own lives. We sometimes think it's simply inborn, and some people are more fortunate than others. The truth is: We are all capable of enjoying our lives and living them with purpose. Every one of us can be happy if we (1) choose happiness, (2) learn and apply happiness principles and tools, and (3) practice happiness every day.

The following habits for practicing happiness are not ranked in any specific order of importance. It is suggested that you start with the principles that are most helpful and important to you.

As you consistently practice these principles, you will start to see positive changes that occur in your attitude and life. An increase in joy and a lifestyle of true and lasting happiness can be yours!

HABIT #1: Practice happiness...with a new perspective
Pessimists & Optimists See Things Differently

Do you usually focus on what you have or what is missing?
Do you think about what you need or what you're blessed with?

Do you think about what is going good or what is going bad?
Do you point out the negatives or do you look for the positives?
Do you find things to criticize or things to compliment?

HABIT #2: Practice happiness...with the words we speak
Your Words Determine Your Destiny

The words we speak reveal a lot about us—our attitudes, beliefs, feelings, and expectations. Our words not only communicate what we want others to hear, but they have the power to influence and make a real impact on people and situations. We can use our words to encourage and motivate just as we can use them to weaken or defeat ourselves and others.

Every day we have the opportunity to speak what is in our hearts and on our minds. Oftentimes, we don't even think about what we're going to say. And, we don't take the time to reflect on it. As we do, we will learn how our manner of speech contributes to our happiness.

HABIT #3: Practice happiness...by living in the present
Living in the Past, Present, or Future

Physically we live in the present moment. Our hearts beat steadily without any effort on our part. Our bodies function to keep us alive from moment to moment. However, our minds aren't always in synch with the here and now. They tend to wander off into the future or back to the past, forfeiting the experience of the present. The present is the only time we have to enjoy. It's the only place happiness exists. We have no control over time. We can't speed it up or slow it down. We can only live it fully now. Right now is the time to be happy.

HABIT #4: Practice happiness...with a thankful heart
What is so Good about Life, Anyway?

We will never encounter a happy person without a heart of gratitude.
A thankful heart is truly a merry heart. The key is believing that life is good, and we share in its goodness. Every day we're presented with opportunities to be thankful for something or someone.

Oftentimes, blessings are taken for granted or overlooked altogether. We get our focus on what we don't have instead. And we miss the simple, everyday goodness in our lives that can bring us much joy.

Recognizing, appreciating, and enjoying a loving hug, help with a chore, a new home furnishing, ability to pay a bill, and so forth can help us develop a daily habit of gratitude. A heart of gratitude happens one blessing at a time

HABIT #5: Practice happiness...by giving and helping others
The More You Give the More You Get

We have all been in positions of being the giver or the taker. Both positions can be a mutually beneficial way of making the world a better place. For the takers—they might get their needs or wants met. For the givers, they might reap the benefits of gratification and happiness. However, our attitudes in giving determine how much joy and gratification we experience. We might give grudgingly or because we feel pressured to give. We might be eager and cheerful to give. We might give freely and from our hearts. We might give with no strings attached. Or, we might have certain expectations and conditions in our giving. How much or how little we give or help others isn't what determines our happiness in doing so. It's our heart in giving that makes the difference.

HABIT #6: Practice happiness...by pursuing inner peace
Finding Shelter in the Storms of Life

We usually don't think of peace and life's storms coexisting. Problems have a way of threatening our inner calm regardless of what is going on around us. Anyone can feel secure and strong when everything is going well. It's inner peace we seek. This kind of peace exists in a calm and undivided mind where assurance and trust are beyond oneself. We can have abiding peace no matter what is going on around us.

HABIT #7: Practice happiness...by living with purpose
What Are You Living For?

We can all live with purpose because there is so much to live for. There are things we can pursue, discover, or accomplish that fill our lives with meaning and purpose. We can have vision for our lives, dream dreams, and fulfill our callings. There is always something for us to do. Pursuing interests, developing skills, setting goals, and prioritizing our time all help us to grow and give us something to anticipate. We can make each day count and live with purpose.

HABIT #8: Practice happiness...by caring for our health
The Body and Mind Connection

Sometimes we take for granted that our minds and bodies are closely connected. When we feel good physically, we are much more likely to feel good mentally and vise versa. We have more energy, motivation, and stamina when we take proper care of our bodies. Our self-esteem is improved when we feel good about our bodies and like the way we look. To a great extent, our daily choices are a major contributing factor to our physical and mental health. Our thought life, perspective, and attitudes play a major role in our mental health.

Our minds and bodies respond to the way we care for them through proper nutrition, exercise, stress management, rest, and relaxation. We have the opportunity to treat our bodies with proper respect, enhance how they perform and look, and be happy with this amazing body we live in. We also have the opportunity to take good care of our minds by guarding our thought life, improving our outlook, changing negative patterns, and increasing our own overall happiness.

HABIT #9: We Live to Love Practice happiness...by loving others
What is life without love?

The source of true happiness and fulfillment can always be traced back to love in one way or another. More than anything else, love is sought after in our lives—within our relationships, occupations; within ourselves. Love gives life meaning and purpose. It fulfills the deepest yearnings of the soul. It quenches our thirst and fills our hearts to overflowing. Love turns darkness to light. Love brings harmony and order out of chaos. Love heals wounds and brings comfort to hurts and pain. Love holds families together. It bonds friendships. Love inspires, revives, and restores

Being In The 'Now' - This Moment Is All We Have and Will Ever Have

Life is the present moment. It is what is unfolding NOW. It is not the past because that it dead. Nor is it the future, for how do I know that I will be there to greet it? No, life is the present; it is all we have. Here's how Nigerian master drummer Babatunde Olatunji explains the same idea, "Yesterday is history. Tomorrow is a mystery. And today? Today is a gift. That's why we call it the present."

Imagine being unfortunate enough to live in a country engulfed by war. Imagine a powerful enemy dropping huge bombs that destroy buildings and life. Imagine building fragments, shards of glass, and shrapnel flying everywhere. Would you voluntarily place yourself in such a hellhole? Yet, look at what we do. We blow the PRESENT MOMENT to smithereens, leaving nothing behind but rubble. And what are the weapons we use to destroy it? Some of our favorite weapons are anger, shame, and regrets. Whenever we experience them we are dwelling in the past. On such occasions, we have abandoned the present, which is life, for the past, which is nonexistence. Other major weapons we use to annihilate the present are fear, anxiety, and worry. When we experience such emotions, we desert the present moment to take up residence in the imaginary future.

Suppose I stop for lunch and as I eat, my mind focuses on how I believe I have been betrayed, embarrassed, or hurt. Where am I at such a time? I am no longer in the restaurant, no longer seated before a delicious meal, no longer surrounded by interesting people. Where am I? I am in the past. I am among the dead. I have destroyed the present moment. The aroma of roast beef and potatoes has been eradicated by resentment. The clatter of dishes, the background music, and the laughter of the people at the table behind me goes unheard because of past hurts that occupy my mind. The texture and beautiful pattern of the tablecloth goes unnoticed as I leave the present and shift my attention to things I am afraid may happen in the future.

The ideas I am now sharing are hardly new. For in addition to introducing the concept of monotheism, the Egyptian pharaoh Akhenaton (1352 ~ 1336 BC, the predecessor of Tutankamen, and husband of Nefertiti) had this to say, "Labor not after riches first, and think thou afterwards wilt enjoy them. He who neglecteth the present moment, throweth away all that he hath."

Don't run from the present and hide in the past or future, for neither is a refuge. No, they are not havens, but prisons. Instead of running, face the present. Become a surfer. Whether you surf or not, pretend for a moment that you are at the ocean. You run into the water, leap on your board, and paddle out to a ground swell. What awaits you? Will it be a bumpy ride or smooth sailing?

Will you be able to climb the face of the approaching wave? Will you have the exhilarating experience of riding inside the 'tube'? Or will you have an 'acid drop' (have the bottom fall out as you free fall down the face of a wave)? Imagine facing wave after wave. Each one unique. Each one promising a new challenge. Each one offering a new adventure. Surfers live in the present and their hearts are full of joy. Become a surfer. Welcome each moment (wave) that comes your way. Delight in the waves of challenges that sweep toward you and ride their crests, for they will carry you to the shore of joy.

Here are a few more points to consider:

1. Remember, no matter what the future has in store, it cannot take away what we have in the present moment. The only thing that can steal it is our own inattention. Neither can past pains and regrets rob us of the joy of the present moment, unless we allow them to do so. Henry Ward Beecher (1813 ~ 1887) adds, "No matter what looms ahead, if you can eat today, enjoy the sunlight today, mix good cheer with friends today, enjoy it and bless God for it. Do not look back on happiness - or dream of it in the

future. You are only sure of today; do not let yourself be cheated out of it."

2. The magic of NOW is that it is the moment of power. Do I wish to change for the better? I can only do that NOW. Do I want to drop a bad habit or start a good one? I can only do that NOW. Do I wish to achieve a goal? I can only do that now. We cannot change our lives in the past. Nor can we change them in the future, for it isn't until the future becomes the present that we can change. So, to live in the past or future is to deny ourselves of great power.

3. When you worry about the future, you are building a house of anxiety. When you regret the past, you erect a house of depression. Return to the present. Wouldn't you rather be enjoying yourself (IN JOY IN YOURSELF)? Let this Sanskrit verse be your guide, "Each today, well-lived, makes yesterday a dream of happiness and each tomorrow a vision of hope. Look, therefore, to this one day, for it and it alone is life."

4. True, the new day may bring a challenge. But as Robert Louis Stevenson (1850 ~ 1895) reminds us, "Anyone can carry his burden, however hard, until nightfall. Anyone can do his work, however hard, for one day. Anyone can live sweetly, patiently, lovingly, purely, until the sun goes down. And this is all that life really means." Every day is just one day, isn't it?

5. If you find yourself in a moment of stress, pressure, or tension, immediately stop what you're doing, take a deep breath, and say to yourself, "I am okay NOW. I am fine NOW. I am in control NOW." Take a ten second break to tune in to the beauty, magic, and wonder of the moment. When you imagination tries to convince you that you are overwhelmed by too much work, just remind it you are a surfer, up to the task. So, leap back into the ocean and ride that wave.

The Objective Observer - Lose Your Identification with Self

"To be identified with your mind is to be trapped in time: the compulsion to live almost exclusively through memory and anticipation." Eckhart Tolle

The fictitious self is an illusion. Any image of self that is identified with any form is ultimately an illusion. The world cannot make you happy - you'll not find lasting satisfaction there. (Only temporary).

Once we learn not to identify with our form, or our Ego, we become free. We can practice the art of becoming an objective observer, without emotion or attachment, and realize we can really start to be free of the madness that is our current state of collective unconsciousness.

A Simple Exercise
First, sit comfortably and relax the body, keeping your arms and legs uncrossed to symbolize bodily your openness. Do not slouch down as there may be a tendency to fall asleep. Try to sit relatively straight without being rigid, and put your body in a position of relaxed alertness.

The next step is called disidentification. The idea is that you have a body. It is a very precious instrument, but you are not your body. You are more than your body. If you think that you are your body, then when your body changes, you lose your identity. The process of disidentification and identification goes on automatically throughout life often with painful consequences. Psychosynthesis teaches us that we can control this process and be in charge of our identities. We can participate in our own evolution by practicing disidentification.

The next step is disidentification from your emotions. Our language tends to reinforce emotional identification. I am angry.

I am afraid, etc. You do have emotions, and they can overcome you with their intensity, but they are not you. They are constantly changing, but you remain. This can be a most significant management tool. As you are able to disidentify from your emotions, you are more able to experience your own center.

Disidentification is not suppression but a recognition that you have these emotions, but you can choose how you wish to express them. This is different from the normal management attitude of repression of emotions. From the centered position you can observe your emotions, consider the alternatives and express ourselves appropriately. There is a great sense of power associated with this experience. This is not the usual form of power where you control others or suppress yourself but a sense of power of the self who is in charge. One is no longer victim of someone pushing your button.

The next step involves disidentification from the mind. For many people this is the most difficult step. Our minds have been very available to us. Our ideas are so important that we tend to believe that we are our minds. Any assault upon our ideas is seen to be an assault on us. For people who have not experienced their own mind, this can be a valuable identification. As many people are identified with their emotions, a step in growth for them is to begin to identify with their minds.

At the level of awareness that we are dealing with, where the mind is well developed, the next step in growth will be to disidentify from the mind and identify with the personal self. The mind has been in charge, and now it is time to tell it who is the boss. "I affirm that I have a mind, but I am more than my mind. I value it. I use it. I can choose to think the way that I wish to think. I am not ruled by my ideas about life, but I keep an open mind, integrating new awarenesses about reality when they conflict with familiar long-held beliefs. I can let go of old ideas if they become limiting or inaccurate in the light of new experience."

As we complete this process of disidentification, we begin to identify with the personal self. We experience our self--our own center. Surrounding you are your instruments for functioning in the world. We choose our actions, our feelings, our thoughts. This is the essence of personal psychosynthesis, and a major trait of the self-actualizer.

Centering Exercise

Take the time to center yourself and focus in. We will do this basic psychosynthesis exercise. Quiet yourself and sit in a comfortable position. Close your eyes. You are going to disidentify, stepping back from the various parts of yourself in order to get to the center--the personal self--the observer that is beyond any of your individual parts. This self is the integrative factor that coordinates all aspects of the personality. So just step away from the parts starting with the body.

I have a body, but I am more than my body. I am the one who is aware: the self, the center. My body may be rested or tired, active or inactive, but I remain the same, the observer at the center of all my experience. I am aware of my body, but I am more than my body.

I have emotions, but I am more than my emotions. Whether I feel excited or dull, I recognize that I am not changing. I have emotions, but I am more than my emotions.

I have an intellect, but I am more than my intellect. Regardless of my thoughts and regardless of how my beliefs have changed over the years, I remain the one who is aware, the one who chooses--the one who directs my thinking process. I have an intellect, but I am more than that.

I am a center of pure awareness. I am the one who chooses. I am the self.

Through the process of disidentification you become more and more your own manager. You find yourself becoming more free from concerns about the expectations or judgments of other people. The self is the inner director.

Another effect of disidentification is the development of a discrimination between being centered versus being off center. Most people cannot do this because they do not have the experience of being centered. As you begin to experience being centered, there is a tendency to experience a sense of permanence. At the center there is stability. Even though the environment is changing you are identified in that stable center

Helping Others

Longest Running Study Shows Helping Others Makes Us Happy

Laura Goodall believes she has a great life. But it hasn't been easy. Her father deserted her mother when Laura was in high school. She suffers from chronic arthritis and psoriasis. She was 47 when her husband left her and their five teen-aged children-after divesting himself of all financial assets, so Goodall was ordered by the court to vacate their home and pay him half her teacher's salary. Her older brother was killed in an airplane crash, and though she was still struggling financially, she often took in a nephew or two to live with her.

Why does Laura Goodall consider her life to have been so wonderful? She's remarried, close to all her children, a practicing Catholic whose faith enlivens her life, and above all, she feels joy in giving to others. She and her second husband run a nature store. "We feel very good about what we're doing," she says, "trying to make people aware how fortunate we are to have this beautiful world. It's always been important to me that I've done something I thought would contribute to society."

Goodall is one of nearly 200 individuals followed by psychologists for the last half-century as part of one of the longest-running social-science studies of our time. The research, which began in Oakland, California, in the 1920s, combined semi-annual interviews until participants graduated from high school, and has since followed them at intervals of 10 years. An astounding 90 percent of people have stayed in the study, giving it coherence and offering insights into what constitutes a happy life. One of the keys is generativity-the ability to give to others-according to psychologist and researcher Paul Wink of Wellesley College, who oversees the study and has co-authored a book on the findings titled In the Course of a Lifetime.

"Laura is absolutely happy and vital," says Wink. "She manages to turn everything that happens to her into a good event. When she got a very bad ear infection recently she felt that it would help her understand the deaf-she actually said she'd gained 'a totally, beautifully, new understanding of deaf people.' She describes everything in generative terms-in terms of giving to others."

According to Wink, the protective effect of giving on mental and physical health buffers an entire lifetime. Wink found that teens who scored high on generativity in high school were healthier and happier half a century later. "There was a strong correlation with mental health in particular," he says.

Wink has interviewed more than 90 of the study participants all over the U.S., while a colleague has interviewed the rest and produced videotapes for Wink to watch. He's been mining all the data to sift out the health effects of generativity and faith, and hopes for funding to study how these folks develop wisdom. "I rarely have found such interesting data," he marvels. "The lives of these people span all the major changes of the 20th century.

They were children in the Great Depression, teens during World War II-establishing families and careers at the height of the post-war suburban boom, and hitting midlife during the turmoil of the 1960s and 1970s. Now at the turn of the 21st century, they're living in a high-tech, multicultural society marked by global trade, the Internet and worldwide geopolitical tensions." In short, lives that encompass so much change have incredible breadth-nevertheless, the study is unusually consistent because the same questions were asked of these individuals again and again over the course of decades.

So what's the key to generativity? Wink explains, "Generativity can't exist unless you have the sense that you can make a difference. We've found that empathy and warmth are important, so that you can feel the suffering of others. And it's equally important to have a desire to give and help. But what leads the way is a healthy sense of self that allows you to mobilize and act productively upon the world."

Generativity is also linked to faith-both organized religion and a kind of autonomous spirituality that may take diverse forms. Wink compared the impact of traditional religion and a more eclectic, diffuse spirituality that might encompass meditation, Eastern religion and shamanism. Both score equally well for instilling generativity in people, but more traditionally religious individuals see altruism and giving as the natural outpouring of their faith, while for more eclectic spiritual seekers, generativity includes a desire to effect others or to pass on worthwhile skills and knowledge.

"The generativity of spiritual seekers," says Wink, "includes a strong, self-expansive focus on making creative contributions that will affect others and endure beyond their lifetimes."

But in the end, the why doesn't matter so much as the act of giving, which not only benefits others, but boosts the health of those like Laura Goodall, who at age 80 is still living a rich, vital life. In the end, says Wink, "the thought [that] the way you behave at the age 16 can relate to your health at age 70 is really exciting.

Part of true happiness involves being of service. Being of service to others. Being of service means helping others. Your personal fulfillment involves you being of service to others.

Without that factor, without being of service and helping others, you will never feel totally happy, you will always feel incomplete and somewhat unfulfilled, as if "something" is missing from your life. Being of service, helping others, is a large and important part of higher and deeper happiness and complete fulfillment.

There are many ways you can help others. Being of service to others can take many forms and can be active or passive. Active service can be volunteering or donating your time through organizations that help others. You could volunteer at your local soup kitchen, homeless shelter, Salvation Army, Red Cross, hospital or one of the many charitable organizations in your area. Or you could donate money. Or you could make an effort to help people directly, by being available to people who need help and could benefit from your talents and experience and expertise. Lawyers do this when they supply their legal services pro bono, for free.

Each of us has a unique and special talent for something. Each of us has something that we love to do, that we do exceptionally well. That something, that natural talent and ability, is a good thing to use in helping others. And, in doing that, in helping others, you will be fulfilled, you will fulfill your higher purpose in life. It's not always about having professional experience and expertise or special education in a given field (such as law, medicine, finance, etc.), it's about helping others.

Throughout my life people have approached me for advice or understanding of their problems. I help them by understanding their problem, clarifying it, and exploring possible solutions with them.

Apparently, I am good at this and have a natural talent for it, as people keep seeking me out for this. Including strangers. I have no formal training for it, do not do it for money and am careful not to render legal, medical or other licensable advice. Over my lifetime I have helped hundreds, maybe thousands, of people in this way.

It seems to work; after talking with me about their problem they go away feeling better. This is how I am of service to others, how I help others, how I fulfill my true purpose in life. And, I also write articles and books that can reach and help MORE people understand and improve their life. Or, in the case of this book, achieve the goal of life; happiness. What do I get from doing this, from being of service to others? A lot. I get a lot of satisfaction, a lot of happiness and I am fulfilling my life purpose.

"Everyone has a purpose in life ... a unique gift or special talent to give to others. And when we blend this unique talent with service to others we experience the ecstasy and exultation of our own spirit, which is the ultimate goal of all goals." --Deepak Chopra

However you are of service to others, do it gladly, do it selflessly, do it whenever you can. The reward you get for helping others, for being of service to others, is fulfillment ... a deep sense of purpose and happiness.

Being of service to others, helping others, can make YOU happy. And it can change the world.

Freeing The Mind

In a primitive existence, where threats to life are common, it is wise to set up procedures which give us advanced warning of danger and which present us with fearful mental pictures or sounds, which motivate us to escape or attack before the real threat emerges.

If these procedures are so powerful that they shut down the conscious, thinking mind and work our bodies like a reflex - independently of our conscious thinking and will - and automatically put us into a fight or flight mode with all the fear and panic that gives us energy then this may a small price to pay for survival.

That is, it may have been helpful in caveman times. In fact, it probably was. Even if this meant we have lots of false alarms. Because of the danger it is worth it. It's better to jump a few times a day than be devoured by tigers!

Notice flocks of birds, how they panic many times a day at the slightest sign of danger. But for us, in modern society, such responses no longer needed. They may even prevent us from attaining what we want, and reduce us to mere automata. In fact, they probably do.

Freeing ourselves of these ancient or childish ways of thinking and acting and remodeling, we can learn to respond better. If a hungry tiger suddenly appears, and looks at us greedily, then a split-second reflexive response with extreme fear (to energize us) and fight, flight or feigning death would be appropriate.

If the boss looks at us fiercely, this panic response, designed for tigers does not help. Bosses do not normally pounce on people and begin to eat them! And under these circumstances we need to use our brains, not our emotions! By keeping our heads and communicating wisely, we would certainly do better. What worked in the jungle, does not work in the modern office!

Clean up the mind

By clearing out this mental debris and developing more appropriate ways of thinking, we can free ourselves and regain mastery of our minds. Like the computer designer who has succumbed to his machine, and realizes that he must free himself of its control, we need to free ourselves of our obsolete mental procedures.

In his book Wisdom 2.0, Soren Gordhamer explores a concept he calls cup mind.

The mind, he explains, can be like a cup or the ocean. When you place a drop of blue dye in a cup, the entire contents may change color, whereas when you place that same drop in the ocean, it barely has an impact.

Our thoughts and feelings can affect our minds similarly. They can completely consume us and alter our entire experience of a given day; or, if we create enough mental space, they can be a part of our experience that we can notice, sit with, and then release.

We can allow anger from the morning to snowball in the afternoon and evening, or we can recognize it, feel it, then let it go. We can obsess over everything we think we did wrong or want to do differently, or we can recognize the stress and worry, move beyond them, and then decide to see things from a different angle.

Today if your mind gets overwhelming, ask yourself: What can I do to create some space? Then do it: Take a walk, practice deep breathing, or simply sit in stillness.

We are always going to think and feel. There is no escape from the mind. Whether or not it's a prison is entirely up to us.

Getting Outside the Self and Ego

Whenever we give our power to anything outside of ourselves, we become susceptible to feelings of anguish, anxiety, depression, and stress. Usually the cause can be found when your ego has become attached and strongly identified with the outside world.

Your ego is essentially your self image, it's the mask you display to society. Your ego only survives by constantly seeking approval from that which it wants to identity with. Therefore all the unhappiness you experience comes from the constant battle of your ego seeking approval in the outside world.

You can feel your ego when you become attached and live your world by identifying your identity through the thoughts of:

Praise and Blame: Whenever you receive praise if you are not aware you will become puffed up in your own ego. Whenever the outside world does not go according to the way you would like it, you learn to put your blame on it.

Gain and Loss: Your ego is only concerned with what's in it for me. When you gain something, you are never happy because than you are only worried about loosing it.

Pleasure and Pain: The ego wants to only experience pleasure, but the only pleasure it can receive is momentary in nature, because it needs external things to satisfy its desires. Superficial pleasures are always accompanied by the same amount of pain. At the time we receive extreme pleasure in drinking too much wine with friends, only to regret it the next day.

Fame and Shame: Since your ego only survives by seeking approval from the outside world it concerns it self with becoming happy through fame. You become famous than you worry about not doing anything that will bring you shame. You are never truly at ease with yourself because you worry about how others perceive you and whether it will bring you fame or shame.

When you believe that your identity is your ego, you will only live your world in reactive mode. You will live your life only in direct relation to how you are affected by gain and loss, pleasure and pain, fame and shame. Living like this you will never be living in reality; you are only experiencing this world from the self conscious perspective. By living your life from only a self conscious perspective, you only experience this world from your own thoughts, your living in your own little world disconnected from the greater reality.

If you are not careful you will be lost, if you try and search for happiness, you will never find it because it's not real. Happiness is not something you find outside of yourself. Happiness is something that is already inside you, you have to decide to be happy. You have to realize that happiness will never be found in egoist desires.

Since your ego comes from you memory and can only think of the past and imagine the future, you need to learn to be more present to transcend it. The real you can be felt when you are truly present in whatever you are doing. If you are able to go a park sit on a bench, learn to watch everything that's going on around you, without thinking of the past or imagining the future, you will catch glimpses of your true identity. You must learn to watch whatever is going on inside you with out becoming attached to your thoughts.

The more you do this the more you will develop a calm mind that does not automatically react to the immense number of thoughts we have. Next time you are driving and someone cuts you off, learn to just watch the thoughts that arise, if you do not become attached and give power to them, they will fade away and you will not react by screaming at the driver. It's impossible to separate our selves from our ego, this is by nature how we are designed, learn to understand it, so you can learn from it on your journey to self realization.

Getting Past The Ego

It is important to be fully yourself, and fully present in order to feel the peace and joy at being one with life.

Although this does not sound as if it would be alien to the ego, the ego opposes reality. as Eckhart Tolle says, The ego thrives on unhappiness and negativity. This is the basis of unconscious living -- creating unhappiness and suffering without recognizing it. As Jesus said, "Forgive them for they know not what they do."

Ask yourself, Tolle suggests, "Is there unhappiness in me now?" Attend to any low level unhappiness in any form, such as discontent, nervousness or being "fed up." Thoughts will appear to justify it, but in reality they are causing it.

This is when Ho'oponopono will help. This is an ancient, updated, Hawaiian method of problem solving by clearing. When we feel a feeling or have a thought that is unwarranted or unwanted, we take notice, and then ask Divinity to transmute the memory or program that caused it.

We acknowledge our love and gratefulness for helping to rid us of this thought or feeling; we apologize for having the thought or feeling and ask for forgiveness. "Divinity, please take this thought, memory or feeling and transmute it to the light. Thank you. Please forgive me. I'm sorry. I love you." This is more powerful than you can imagine, although it is simple.

Take the time to connect with Spirit.

Quiet your mind.

All thoughts are ego-speak.

Be in the present.

Attend to where you are and the life around you if you are in a beautiful place. Or, if you are in a place with advertisements and writing everywhere you look (bus, subway or train, crowded city street with billboards or store signs), then sit for a moment and close your eyes until you find the calm within. Breathe deeply and slowly.

Faith

Many people find that faith in God helps them to achieve happiness, so whatever your definition of God is, whether it be a higher power or other belief, if it works for you, you should pursue it.

Today I attended a meeting in which 25 of us discussed the power of the mind, the power of belief, and the power of faith, which we treated as essentially the same thing; mainly, the power our mind (thoughts, opinions, beliefs, attitude) has over our physical and mental health, success, and happiness. I was pleasantly surprised to find everyone in agreement that how we view life creates the life we view.

That is, as someone else once said, "If life is a comedy to him who thinks, and a tragedy to him who feels, it is a victory to him who has faith." After all, if we have a negative attitude, we will experience a negative life (poor health, failures, and unhappiness). Not so long ago, the average person, and even many professionals, scoffed at the idea that the primary cause of man's suffering was the way he viewed life or what he believed in.

But now we know better. For example, Walter R. Newell, Professor of Political Science and Philosophy at Carleton University in Ottawa, Canada wrote, "If we believe the world as a whole is orderly and intelligible, we will behave in the same way. If we believe the world is chaotic and irrational, we will in turn be governed by impulse and passion (emotions)." Clearly, what we put our faith in will determine the quality of our life.

But perhaps I'm getting ahead of myself. Perhaps, before writing about the importance of placing our faith in the right place, I should begin by stressing how important it is to have faith. More than a half century ago, John Foster Dulles (1888~1959) expressed his concern about this matter: "We are establishing an all-time world record in the production of material things. What we lack is a righteous and dynamic faith. Without it, all else avails us little. The lack cannot be compensated for by politicians, however able; or by diplomats, however astute; or by scientists, however inventive; or by bombs, however powerful."

Yes, the answer to the world's problems doesn't lie in bigger threats, bombs, missiles, and armies, but in more faith. Faith in what? Faith in the intrinsic goodness of humanity. Faith in human nature. Faith in our ability to settle disputes peacefully. Our enemies want the same things we do; mainly, security, a sound economy, and respect. When we call our enemies evil, barbaric, and heinous, do we expect them to sit down with us and negotiate? When we strike a dog with a stick, do we expect it to wag its tail, or to lunge at us?

Yes, we need faith. Faith that things can, do, and will change for the better. Faith in ourselves. Faith that we have the necessary inner resources to cope with any difficulty. Faith that nothing is impossible. Faith that problems are the solutions to gaining strength and sharing in the adventure of life. Faith that in the end everything will turn out all right, and if things are not alright now, that's because it is not yet the end.

THE IMPORTANCE OF FAITH

1. It is the source of great strength. I smiled when I read how Walter Lippmann (1889~1974) made this same point: "Men with faith can face martyrdom while those without it feel stricken when they are not invited to dinner." Who are the great achievers? Those with strong faith or those whose hearts are filled with doubt?

Harry Emerson Fosdick (1878-1969) makes a strong case for faith: "Fear imprisons, faith liberates; fear paralyzes, faith empowers; fear disheartens, faith encourages; fear sickens, faith heals; fear makes useless, faith makes serviceable." Reverend Fosdick astutely realized that it is fear, not doubt, that is the opposite of faith. You see, we place our faith or trust in something because we expect good to result, so faith is the expectation of something good. And fear is the expectation of something bad (harmful).

2. Faith is the pillar that supports all acts of creation, or as Henry Miller (1891-1980) put it, "Back of every creation, supporting it like an arch, is faith. Enthusiasm is nothing: it comes and goes. But if one believes, then miracles occur." What is it, other than faith, that prods us along, one step at a time toward our goals? Some say, "I will believe it when I see it." But we will not see it until we first believe it.

3. Reason can go only so far, but faith has no limits. In the past, men of reason (scientists) have said that travel to the moon is impossible. But despite their concerns, men of faith brought us safely to the moon and back.

Would a reasonable person expect a ten year old child to sing opera? But a ten year old girl with faith proved she could do it. If you are one of the few people who haven't seen her yet, you can see Jackie Evancho here.

4. Men and women of faith are free of worry. One of NASA's most brilliant and fearless managers, George E. Mueller agrees, for he said, "The beginning of anxiety is the end of faith, and the beginning of true faith is the end of anxiety." Faith frees us from needless anxiety, fear, and worry, and allows us to focus on what is important.

Five months ago my car was completely destroyed in an accident. Needing another one, I visited a used car dealer. Met a salesman; we chatted, and got acquainted. I asked him which car in the lot was the best. He took me to one that was exactly two years old and in mint condition. He opened the door and gave me the key. I sat down, turned on the ignition, looked at the all-digital instrument panel, turned off the ignition, returned the key, got out of the car, and said, "Let's talk business."

At his desk, he showed me all of the car's documents, and told me how much the dealership was asking for the car. I explained that I wasn't interested in how much they wanted. Rather, I wanted to know how low they would be willing to go to get me to buy the car now. The salesman tried to get me to make an offer first. But I relentlessly refused. At last, he wrote down a figure on a sheet of paper and pushed it toward me, saying, "This is the best I can do."

I looked at the price, crossed it out, wrote a new figure, and while pushing it back to him said, "Give it to me at this price and I will pay for it in cash now." After getting approval from his manager, I got the car.

But I wonder if you got the real point of the story. You see, I paid thousands of dollars in cash for a car I did not test drive. At most, I spent five minutes looking at the car. I'm not suggesting that everyone behave as I did, but I trusted the salesman, had faith in the dealership, believed in the brand (Honda), trusted the documents, and had faith in my judgment and experience. Free from worry, I was able to act quickly and get exactly what I wanted. Five months have passed and my wife and I remain in love with the car.

5. "Faith sees the invisible, believes the unbelievable, and receives the impossible." (Corrie Ten Boom, 1892~1983)

HARNESSING THE POWER OF FAITH

Thankfully, more and more people are recognizing the importance of faith. But simply understanding how important it is, is not enough to release its power. To benefit from its might, you must move beyond mere understanding to making it a part of you. It is not enough to understand the truth of faith; you must make it true for YOU. Only then will you be transformed by this mighty force.

Charles Blondin (1824~1897) was a French tightrope walker and acrobat that moved to the United States and gained fame by crossing the gorge below Niagara Falls on a tightrope, 1100 feet (335 m) long, 3¼ inches in diameter, 160 feet (50 m) above the water, carrying his manager, Harry Colcord on his back. One day, just before starting, he asked someone in the audience if he believed that he could do it.

"Yes," the man replied, "you can do it!"

The Great Blondin asked again, more emphatically.

"Yes, I'm sure you can do it!"

"Good," said Blondin, "because my manager isn't here today and I need you to ride over on my back."

When your faith in yourself, in others, and in life matches that of the faith of Blondin's manager, you will have released the power of faith, and you will be capable of living the life of your dreams.

SOME CHARACTERISTICS OF FAITH

We've come this far without defining faith. It may seem unnecessary, but just to clarify our understanding, I'll make a few points.

1. Faith means confidence, but not certainty, for if the outcome were certain, there would be no need for faith.

2. Faith is a continuation of reason. To have faith in the power of belief is not fancy or wishful thinking. It is reasonable because it is based on reason or science. After all, the placebo effect, or healing that comes from faith in the treatment rather than the treatment itself, is a long established scientific fact.

Tryon Edwards (1809~1894) also makes a good point about the relationship between science and faith, "Science has sometimes been said to be opposed to faith, and inconsistent with it. But all science, in fact, rests on a basis of faith, for it assumes the permanence and uniformity of natural laws - a thing which can never be demonstrated."

For the latest thought on how the mind influences our body and well being and for an introduction to epigenetics and biomolecular medicine see these two books (Don't be afraid; they are written for the layperson):

The Biology of Belief: Unleashing the Power of Consciousness, Matter, & Miracles, Bruce H. Lipton Ph.D. Hay House, 2008.

Molecules Of Emotion: The Science Behind Mind-Body Medicine by Candace B. Pert, Simon & Schuster, 1999

3. Faith is pragmatic. Faith makes sense because it works. To have faith in yourself, humanity, and life leads to success and happiness. The naysayers and doomsday purveyors prove nothing other than their attitude leads to unhappiness.

4. "To one who has faith, no explanation is necessary. To one without faith, no explanation is possible." (St. Thomas Aquinas, 1225~1274)

5. Reason is knowing with our mind; faith is knowing with our heart.

6. "There is no such thing as a lack of faith. We all have plenty of faith, it's just that we have faith in the wrong things. We have faith in what can't be done rather than what can be done. We have faith in lack rather than abundance but there is no lack of faith." (Eric Butterworth, 1916~2003)

7. Faith is patience and persistence; it is holding on to our dream even after our rational mind gives up.

8. Faith is the gateway to adventure, for life is a leap of faith.

9. "Faith is building on what you know is here, so you can reach what you know is there." (Cullen Hightower)

"It's like driving a car at night. You never see further than your headlights, but you can make the whole trip that way." (E. L. Doctorow)

10. Danish philosopher Soren Kierkegaard (1813~1855) adds, "Faith is the highest passion in a human being. Many in every generation may not come that far, but none comes further."

CAVEATS

1. True, when we place our trust in others, we may occasionally be deceived, but better to trust many than to trust none and live in torment.

2. Some wish they had faith, but none who have it wish they didn't.

3. "We seldom lose our faith by a blow out, usually it is just a slow leak." (author unknown) Guard against slow leaks.

4. They who have no faith when the sun is shining will have none when the clouds come.

5. "Just as a small fire is extinguished by the storm whereas a large fire is enhanced by it - likewise a weak faith is weakened by predicament and catastrophes whereas a strong faith is strengthened by them." (Viktor E. Frankl, 1905~1997)

6. Don't seek faith that life will spare you from difficulties. Rather, seek faith that life will give you the strength to overcome anything it throws your way.

HOW DO WE CULTIVATE, MAINTAIN, OR INCREASE OUR FAITH?

1. Focus on what you can do rather than what you can't do.

2. Never say you cannot do something without adding the word "yet." Example: I cannot dance YET.

3. Be open to it. Faith cannot enter a closed mind any more than you can enter a closed room

4. Look for reasons to have faith, not reasons to have doubt. Remember, we find what we look for.

5. Set and work toward your goals. Each success you experience will lead you to believe you are in control and anything is possible.

6. Help others have faith. Remember, we have to give away what we wish to receive.

7. Enjoy inspirational books, magazines, and movies.

8. Associate with positive thinkers, for you will become like the people you hang out with.

9. Don't be afraid to be tested, for a faith that hasn't been tested can't be trusted.

"Pity the human being who is not able to connect faith within himself with the infinite. He who has faith has... an inward reservoir of courage, hope, confidence, calmness, and assuring trust that all will come out well - even though to the world it may appear to come out most badly." (B.C. Forbes, 1880~1954)

The Importance of Community

The human being is a social being. We live in a society and like to share our feelings, happiness and sorrows with our friends, relatives and others. This wish of togetherness and belonging leads to create a community as a whole. Community is a broader term and has a larger connotation.

International research has long documented the connection between community participation and mental health and well-being. Getting more connected and involved with others can improve self esteem, increase a sense of belonging and protect against depression and anxiety.

More recently, studies suggest that the relationship between community participation and mental health and well-being is more complex than first thought. The research suggests that we may require more targeted strategies to promote community participation for different parts of the community e.g. busy working parents, young people, or for men and women.

Usually community refers to a group of people living in a common geographical location. This group of people obeys some social norms and some common value among themselves. As such, there are so many communities the world over, separated by languages, cultures, or geographical locations. However, they are related to each other in some way or other, thus making entire world a one, single community.

A sense of community is important to establish peace and harmony among the society. The division of work, feeling of association, togetherness, and cooperation - all these help in establishing a healthy atmosphere filled with unity, harmony and friendship. The sense of a community is also important in fostering a feeling of intra-national as well as international brotherhood. Let us discuss these points, in an absence of which there will be complete chaos in the community.

Sense of Togetherness
A sense of togetherness lies in the soul of every individual. This comes from our care and dependency on our fellow beings. From our childhood days to our adulthood, we care for our family members, our relatives, our neighbors and friends. This leads to a need of togetherness among people, which helps in creating a community. We tend to enjoy any festival or social ritual together. This is a kind of community feeling. Without community people will be alone, there won't be anyone to talk to or to share with.

Isolation can lead the "monkey-mind" to generate thoughts not connected to reality. Sociopaths often isolate, their minds spinning out imaginary resentments against "them," the society as whole. This dualistic thinking can lead to a complete breakdown of a sense of connectedness to the whole and affect well-being to a profound degree.

Division of Work
We share our work and this division of work leads to our dependency on other people working in different roles. In every walk of our lives, we have to depend on others apart from our family members. For example, the cobbler repairs shoes for us, the barber cuts our hair, tailor stitches fashionable clothes for us, butcher cuts meat for us, bakers prepares biscuits for us, engineers make houses for us, etc. All these individuals fall into a community, without whom our lives will be very difficult. Division of work is, therefore, important for a well-formed and well-functioning community.

Cooperation
The very idea of community comes into being because people like to cooperate with each other. The sense of cooperation begins at home and it leads to a strong feeling of international brotherhood.

Feeling of Association

In a community people live by associating with one another. The feeling of association is a common human feeling. This helps in establishing peace and harmony within a community. Without a feeling of association there will be chaos and disharmony in the society or community. Hence, this point plays an important role in making a lively and vibrant community.

Thus, with all these points in a perfect combination, a community can help in making a peaceful and progressive society. Likewise, any imbalance could give rise to problems that are disrupting peace and harmony the world over.

What is My Purpose?

The meaning of life is a life of meaning. Happiness is about finding your purpose and meaning in life. It's about finding what you love to do the most, living with passion, searching for what gives your life meaning.

It's about being in tune with who you really are and living a life of purpose. Having a purpose in your life is almost like a spiritual experience. The One Question helps you find the answer to the one question we all need an answer for: what should I do with my life?

Until you discover the purpose of your life, you are living a life of mediocrity. Rise and be great, do the great things you were meant to do. Look deep inside you, realize what's your life's purpose and embrace it.

And when you do find purpose and meaning in life, you discover yourself to be a greater person than you ever dreamed yourself to be. The world you live in will never be the same and the opportunities life throws at you will be abundant.

Explore yourself, discover your purpose of life and live your passion.

Getting Involved

A great way to get connected to people and your community is to volunteer to help with a cause that will help people in need.

Volunteering for a worthwhile cause is one of the most rewarding things we can do with our lives. It takes little effort to get involved in community service and the rewards far outweigh the effort. So, use the following information to learn how to get involved in community service.

1. Pick a community service area to volunteer that you are interested in or care deeply about. Think about what your interests are. Perhaps you would like to work with children or are compassionate to the needs of the elderly or animals.

2. Contact a hospital volunteer program if you want to help those having problems due to serious illness. Other options related to health care are nursing homes and senior assisted living areas. Many of these people just need someone to talk to, have someone read to them or share a meal with them. Children's hospitals need people to help read to children and do crafts. There are also community service needs to help those and their families going through the final months of their lives.

3. Talk to your minister, priest or rabbi about needs in your church or temple community. There are always those in need that the church communities know about. Your church may have a food pantry that needs someone to help with collections or getting the foods to those in need. Some churches sponsor clothing and coat collections for those in need as well. You may even be able to organize a food drive, clothing or coat drive to benefit your church or community.

4. Call your local school district to see if there are volunteers needed for community service work within the schools in your area. Schools sometimes need volunteers to read to children that

have special needs or vision problems. There are many other options within schools for community service if you enjoy working with children. Think about putting together a used book sale to benefit the children of your community so they can have new books.

5. Visit your community's animal shelter to what volunteer needs are there. They may need dog walkers, individuals to help with pet adoptions or pet foster programs. You might just make a list of their supply needs and start a community campaign to donate the items or money for the items. Helping animals in your area would be great community service.

6. Have fun while doing community service. Get involved in organizations in your community such as Rotary Clubs, Women Leagues, Junior Women's Guilds, museum committees and even the zoo. These organizations do regular community service events to benefit their communities and have fun while they're doing it. So join the fun and meet other people that want to get involved.

7. Enlist the participation of your co-workers to get involved in community service. Adopt a child or family for Christmas to help a needy family. Get a group of co-workers together to do work on the home of elderly person in your area. Yes, it's work, but it's so rewarding and fun if you do it together.

Mental Exercises

Dorothea Brande was an American writer and editor, well known for her books Wake Up and Live and Becoming a Writer.

In Wake Up and Live, published in 1936, Brande suggests several mental exercises to make your mind keener and more flexible. These exercises are meant to pull you out of your usual habits, give you a different perspective, and put you in situations that will demand resourcefulness and creative problem solving.

Brande argues that only by testing and stretching yourself can you develop mental strength.

Apart from the goals of creativity and mental flexibility, Brande's exercises make sense from a happiness perspective. One thing is clear: novelty and challenge bring happiness. People who stray from their routines, try new things, explore, and experiment tend to be happier than those who don't.

Novelty and challenge can also bring frustration, anxiety, confusion, and annoyance along the way; it's the process of facing those challenges that brings the "atmosphere of growth" that's so important to happiness. (It's the First Splendid Truth: to be happy, you must think about feeling good, feeling bad, and feeling right within an atmosphere of growth.) Here are more of her suggestions:

1. Spend an hour each day without saying anything except in answer to direct questions, in the midst of the usual group, without creating the impression that you're sulking or ill. Be as ordinary as possible. But do not volunteer remarks or try to draw out information.

2. Think for thirty minutes a day about one subject exclusively. Start with five minutes.

3. Talk for fifteen minutes a day without using the words I, me, my, or mine.

4. Pause on the threshold of any crowded room and size it up.

5. Keep a new acquaintance talking about himself or herself without allowing him to become conscious of it. Turn back any courteous reciprocal questions in a way that your auditor doesn't feel rebuffed.

6. Talk exclusively about yourself and your interests without complaining, boasting, or boring your companions.

7. Plan two hours of a day and stick to the plan.

8. Set yourself twelve tasks at random: e.g., go twenty miles from home using ordinary conveyance; go twelve hours without food; go eat a meal in the unlikeliest place you can find; say nothing all day except in answer to questions; stay up all night and work.

9. From time to time, give yourself a day when you answer "yes" to any reasonable request.

Doing these kinds of exercises can seem artificial, but it can also be a fun way to put a little challenge into your ordinary routine.

Meditation - Visualization - Freeing The Mind

Visualization meditation is the best way to refocus your mind to gain the benefits of meditation. With this method you take yourself away from the distracting stressful thoughts and situations of the day.

What is Visualization Meditation?
It is a form of meditation in which you use your imagination to relax your body, mind, and spirit. Visualization is seeing with your mind.

Visualization can change your frame of mind. Your thoughts and feelings project energy and attract energy of a similar nature. The thoughts and feeling from visualizing a calm and tranquil environment will transform that stressful, worried energy, you were holding inside, into a calm and peaceful energy. This is what brings you back to center, the core of your spiritual nature.

Simple Meditation Exercises
In the beginning use a simple visualization meditation technique. Hold an image in your mind's eye. It can be anything from your

favorite flower to the image of a peaceful meadow. As you visualize keep your breathing in its natural rhythm.

Keep it simple until you are able to keep your concentration on the image. If you find your mind wandering just bring it back to the image. This is a good way to practice visualizing.

Visualization Meditation: Discover the Center of Your Being

Begin this meditation by getting comfortable either sitting in the traditional meditation poses with legs crossed and back straight or sitting with a straight back and your feet flat on the floor. You can also lie down if you feel you will not fall asleep.

Take a few deep breaths and with each breath relax into it.

Let's begin:

1. Visualize a beautiful house with a welcoming front porch and a white picket fence around it.

2. As you open the gate and walk along the path to the front porch you enjoy all the lovely flowers in the front yard. You reach the porch and climb the few stairs to the front door.

3. Open the door and find a long hallway lined with pictures of all your favorite people, places, and things. Take time to admire them as you walk down the hall.

4. You come to the end where there is another door and you can see light beaming through it.

5. Open this door into a beautiful candle lit room. You see reflected in the light all the colors of the rainbow and in the center a glowing ball of white light.

6. There may be someone there to greet you; this is your spiritual guide, your inner self.

7. Walk to the center of this glowing ball of light and sit. Just be in this glorious place where everything is as it should be, peaceful and serene.

8. Stay here for as long as you like, perhaps your guide has a message for you or just sit and enjoy the peace and tranquility of your true self, the center of your being where everything is as it should be.

9. When you are ready begin the journey back. Walk through the candle lit room back into the hallway past the pictures of your favorite people, places, and things and out the front door. You pause on the front porch to take a deep breath of fresh garden air then walk down the path to the front gate.

10. Take another deep breath and slowly come back to your physical state.

Physical Exercises for Stress Relief

Exercise for Relieving Stress may be in the form physical, mental, or spiritual exercise - or a combination of all three, e.g. yoga. What is good for the body is good for the mind and vice versa.

Physical exercise is one of the most effective ways of relieving stress. Exercising the body regularly is very effective in managing stress, on its own or as a part of a stress management plan. Getting into better shape improves your mental health as well as your physical health.

When we physically exert ourselves, the body releases chemical substances (endorphins) that are similar in nature to opiates. These natural substances produced by our own bodies are free of side effects, except for making us feel good.

When it comes to stress management, every little bit of exercise counts. Don't think if you can't commit to a stringent fitness routine that it's useless. It's not. What motivates people to do more of something is to do little of something.

Exercises to Suit Everyone

From doing gentle stretching exercises to keeping up in a physically demanding aerobics class, stress relief can be achieved through a wide range of activities. Some people enjoy the solitude of walking alone. Other people need the stimulation of interacting with others, whether walking in a group, participating in a yoga class or other fitness class, or playing a sport such as tennis, racquetball, etc. Interacting with other people during exercise can provide additional stress relief.

Exercise in a Natural Environment Provides Additional Stress Relieving Benefits

Obviously it is more relaxing to walk along a nature trail than to walk along a busy street. Natural surroundings trigger relaxation responses deep in the brain. Even mentally picturing being surrounded by mountains, trees, or watching the waves roll in at the beach can have this calming effect.

*Exposure to daylight also has positive effects on mood - another benefit of exercising outdoors.

Aerobics

Any activity that gets your heart pumping (aerobic exercise) will get those endorphins flowing and relieve stress. Though you should check with your doctor before embarking on any exercise program, walking is usually safe for anyone.

Try to get your heart going a little faster for at least 15 minutes a day. Even a few minutes here and there of brisk walking can provide stress relief and improve your overall health.

Strengthening Exercises

Though not generally as effective as aerobics for relieving stress, many people find that getting into a strengthening exercise program does relieve stress.

Strength exercises are also important to prevent injury during aerobic exercise by strengthening the muscles that support your joints. A toned body has as much impact on mental wellness as physical wellness.

Stretching Exercises
Stretching exercises stimulate receptors in the nervous system that decrease the production of stress hormones. Stretching exercises also relax tight, tense muscles and increase blood flow to the muscles.

Mind-Body Exercises
Yoga exercises involve the body, mind and spirit. Yoga poses improve flexibility and strength and incorporate breathing techniques that aid in relaxation and general wellness.

Stress relief exercises that don't involve movement but involve both mind and body include meditation exercises and deep breathing exercises - both have been shown to reduce blood pressure.

Self-Indulging Activities Alleviate Stress
On the days you don't exercise, do something else you find relaxing - whether getting some massage therapy, soaking away stress in a soothing aromatherapy bath, etc.

Your health is important. It is not selfish to spend time on yourself! How can you have the energy to take care of others unless you take care of your self?

Make fitness a priority. Exercise effectively relieves depression and anxiety. Find an activity that you enjoy and feel the stress melt away. Relieving Stress by exercise, especially aerobic exercise, has been proven to be highly effective.

Music - How Relaxation Music Works

Most people intuitively understand that music can play a powerful role in helping set the mood or reflecting our current state of feeling. Understanding some of the ways music accomplishes this will enable us to use music as a tool. Music as a tool to facilitate relaxation is effective for several definable reasons. I would like to outline some of these basic properties and functions of music as it is used to aid in relaxation.

In our fast-paced world finding time for relaxing has become a major priority. Sometimes we only have a small window of opportunity to try and wind down or take a short break. Music can help by facilitating induction to relaxation. Just as our attention is immediately turned towards finding the flag when we hear the National Anthem being played, selected music can shift our attention of focus away from the hustle and bustle and towards the purpose of relaxing.

As our focus changes to listen to the music, the rhythm of the music begins to establish parameters for our breathing. Breathing is a major component for any relaxation protocol and one of the first things that we can control in trying to begin relaxing. Music may also begin to effect changes in the autonomic body systems including heart rate and blood pressure. Over time and practice, selected music can become a cue for relaxation, a conditioned stimulus that sets the mind and body onto a course for relaxation.

Once the direction has been established in inducing relaxation, music has an important role in maintaining the setting for relaxation to continue. The music holds the focus of attention and may mask unwanted environmental sounds. Appropriate music selections will assist in slowing breathing and taking deep breaths. The rhythm and constant underlying pulse of sedative music selections are mental guidelines for breathing and progressively relaxing each part of the body.

Heart rate and other indicators should remain steady and at a reduced count, especially as repeated practice with the same or similar music has established a conditioned response. The music, especially a well chosen melody, may also lead to positive emotional associations and allow for feelings of self-worth and affirmations.

Music to help in relaxation is best used when combined with other relaxation methods and protocols. As previously outlined, music is a good cue for relaxation and framework for maintaining a relaxed state for a defined period of time. Techniques such as progressive muscle relaxation, deep breathing, circular breathing, imagery or biofeedback are extremely effective when used in conjunction with music.

Experiment with different tempos, rhythms and melodies to gain the full advantage of using music to help structure the relaxation experience. An ascending and then descending melodic scale may lend itself to deep breathing, for example. Some melodies and instrumental arrangements can help set the stage for painting a mental picture of a beautiful nature scene where worries and stress can melt away.

Humor Therapy - How A Funny Outlook Can Free You

The healing properties of laughter have been extolled since biblical times; in the book of Proverbs, you'll find this advice: "A merry heart doeth good like a medicine" [source: Brody]. When it comes to modern day laughter therapy, however, you'll want to consider the book of Cousins. More precisely, the tome "Anatomy of an Illness (As Perceived by the Patient)," written by Norman Cousins in 1979.

Humor can also aid doctor-patient relationships. When Cousins was diagnosed with ankylosing spondylitis, he was given very slim odds of recovery. He was unable to move and in constant pain. However, in the midst of this dire situation, Cousins didn't lose his sense of humor. He credits his recovery to a prescription of "Candid Camera" episodes, Marx Brothers movies and funny stories read by nurses. With 10 minutes of laughter, he wrote, two hours of pain-free sleep could be procured.

Since then, numerous studies have found that while laughter isn't necessarily the best medicine, it's pretty darn good. For example, a study conducted at UCLA found that watching funny shows increased children's tolerance for pain, which could be helpful when tiny patients have to undergo big procedures [source: UCLA]. At the University of Maryland, researchers found that groups that watched humorous films experienced an increase in blood flow compared to groups that watched downers

That could be because laughter has been called internal jogging, and it may confer all the psychological benefits of a good workout [source: Brody]. The act of laughing stimulates hormones called catecholamines, which in turn release the happy juice -- endorphins. With endorphins surging through our bloodstream, we're more apt to feel happy and relaxed. With each laugh, therefore, we're relieving stress, reducing anxiety and increasing our stores of personal energy. All of these psychological and physiological results are wonderful tools in coping with illness, a hospital stay or even just a cranky coworker.

But if you're facing cancer, battling depression, or dealing with the meanest boss on the planet, can anything truly seem funny?

Humor is highly subjective -- what gives one person the giggles might just as easily put another to sleep. Part of laughter therapy is figuring out exactly what tickles your funny bone, so that getting some healing laughs can be just as easy as popping in a DVD. Have no fear about dealing with a curmudgeon who disdains the wit of Woody Allen or those madcap Muppets, though. Proponents of laughter therapy don't limit themselves just to jokes.

Fake laughter can be just as effective as real laughter, meaning that a laughter therapy session is just as likely to involve that zany Garfield as it is to involve a laughter coach imploring you to pretend your arms are paws and roar with laughter.

Or perhaps you'll be invited to exercise some lawnmower laughter, in which you pretend to start up a mower with a few warm-up chuckles, eventually revving up to powerful laughter. People who lead laughter therapy sessions have found that these fake laughs usually give way to the real kind.

Figuring out what makes you happy, as well as cultivating the ability to find humor and laughter in everyday situations, can relieve the stress and tension that comes with life's challenges. Let's say you get devastating news, like a cancer diagnosis. You can choose to be miserable and sink into a depression that will only make fighting cancer harder.

By choosing to laugh and foster happiness, you'll have more energy to fight, and you don't have to put your life on hold due to disease. It holds true for everything from disease to an assignment to work with your worst nemesis -- when you find ways to laugh and be happy, you remain in control, even if it seems like everything else is out of your hands.

If you think there are some things in life that simply can't be laughed away, consider the story of Annette Goodheart. Goodheart was sexually molested as a child, married an alcoholic and indulged her demons with compulsive overeating.

She credits laughter with her recovery and now, armed with her Ph.D., Goodheart counsels others on how to laugh through pain. She doesn't tell jokes, but rather provides space for her patients to laugh, even when society would rather we keep a stiff upper lip.

We all know people who are wound too tightly, who are holding on to past pain. Laughter can help those people loosen their grip and begin to let go of what's bothering them. Researchers at Texas A&M University found that humor leads to increased hopefulness [source: Texas A&M University].

The researchers believe that laughter can help fight negative thoughts in the brain, and with an increase of positive emotions, people begin to see a way out of their misery. Free from the shackles of negativity, people begin to see how to form a plan of attack to deal with the given situation.

Instead of wallowing in embarrassment, consider how falling down the stairs in front of everyone could be turned into a funny anecdote. Laughing at things that hurt can be cathartic and serve as a way for people to regain control over situations that left them feeling powerless.

Even a chuckle after being admonished by a rude police officer can help you to let go of the small stuff. While we could all afford to take life a little less seriously, there are a few instances to tread carefully with laughter therapy.

Using humor that could be construed negatively, such as sarcasm, can do further damage. It's also important to consider the willingness of your patient -- not everyone is ready to let loose with the ho-ho-ho's as soon as they arrive in the hospital. It may be more suitable in the aftermath of a crisis or in a recovery situation

So, before you get yourself all worked up over something that seems like the end of the world, consider whether it wouldn't be easier to see what's playing on Comedy Central. With a few good laughs, your cable bill can double as your therapist's bill.

Movies and TV - Input Affects Output - What You Watch, Listen to and Experience Makes A Difference

Every moment of every day we are bombarded with a staggering amount of input and stimuli. From the internet to television to ringing cell phones, we are not really equipped from an evolutionary point of view to handle the amount of input we receive.

Our electrical circuits are in a state of constant overload, and this contributes to our sense of dissonance and unease, even if only on a subconscious level.

Moreover, the things we choose to watch, such as television and movies and even our choices of music and reading material, all contributes to programming our minds which are essentially supercomputers.

What you put in affects what goes out - as in any energy system.

Make a conscious effort to reduce the amount of sensory input you receive, whenever possible.

Try to make the sensory input you receive soothing and relaxing, and the sensory input be of a positive nature.
Rather than putting the TV on and watching the news, which is stressful much of the time, why not put on relaxing, soothing music?

Or, how about simple silence?

Or even a self-improvement CD?

Similarly, watching television shows and movies depicting violence and dramatizing stressful dramatic situations not only increases your stress and anxiety level, but programs unhappiness into your psyche.

Pursuing Happiness Each Day

Happiness doesn't need to be created for us.

It exists within us, and it's up to us to choose happiness.

Happiness is attainable by anyone, so long as they want it. If you don't want to be happy you won't be. If you really want to change your life and find the happiness you've been searching for, you can do just that!

A great way to find happiness in each day is to give yourself permission to dwell on the positive instead of the negative. It takes practice, but once you become skilled at it, the rewards are pure joy!

Recommended Reading:

The Art of Happiness: A Handbook for Living - Dalai Lama

How To Meditate: The Use-Anywhere Guide To Eliminating Stress and Worry Through Relaxation and Meditation - Steven Williams Chopra, MD.

Ancient Wisdom - Modern World Advice For Better Living From Sages Through the Ages: The Philosophers Handbook Gopi L. Vishnu, Ph.D.

The Power of Now: A Guide to Spiritual Enlightenment - Eckhart Tolle

A New Earth: Create a Better Life - Eckhart Tolle

The Pursuit of Happiness - David G. Myers

Stress Relieving Music:

Music for Relaxation and Deep Meditation
http://www.cdbaby.com/cd/mindwaves

Recommended Websites:

How To Meditate Easily
http://how-to-meditate-easily.com/